Unlocking AI:

A Beginner's Guide to the

Intelligence of Tomorrow

E. Psaila

Unlocking AI: A Beginner's Guide to the Intelligence of Tomorrow

First Edition: **February 2025**

ISBN: 978-1-923432-34-5

Table of Contents

Appendices

Chapter 1: Welcome to the World of AI

Welcome to the fascinating world of Artificial Intelligence! In this opening chapter, we invite you to embark on a journey that spans from science-fiction dreams to the tangible innovations shaping our everyday lives. Whether you're new to the concept of AI or just curious about its potential, this chapter will help you understand why AI is not only transforming technology but also redefining what it means to be human in the modern age.

The New Frontier: AI in Our Lives

Imagine waking up to a smart alarm that adjusts to your sleep cycle, enjoying a breakfast prepared by a robot chef, or even having your car drive you safely through traffic—all without you lifting a finger. These scenarios, which once belonged solely to the realm of futuristic movies and novels, are becoming part of our reality. AI, at its core, is about empowering machines to perform tasks that require human-like intelligence, from learning and problem-solving to recognizing speech and images.

The advances in AI have moved quickly from theoretical discussions to real-world applications. Today, AI touches nearly every aspect of our lives:

- **Healthcare:** AI-powered diagnostic tools help doctors detect diseases at early stages.

- **Finance:** Automated systems analyze market trends and manage investments with impressive precision.

- **Entertainment:** From personalized recommendations on streaming platforms to interactive gaming, AI makes experiences more engaging.

- **Everyday Convenience:** Virtual assistants like Siri and Alexa simplify our daily routines by understanding and responding to our commands.

Why AI Matters for Tomorrow

At first glance, AI might seem like a buzzword thrown around in tech circles, but its implications extend far beyond trendy conversations. AI is fundamentally altering how we interact with the world and how the world interacts with us. Here are a few reasons why AI is essential for our future:

1. **Innovation and Efficiency:** AI helps us solve complex problems faster than ever before. By automating routine tasks and optimizing processes, it frees up human potential for more creative and strategic endeavors.

2. **New Opportunities:** As AI technologies continue to develop, they open doors to new industries and job roles. Understanding AI today prepares you for the

workforce of tomorrow.

3. **Improved Decision-Making:** AI systems can analyze vast amounts of data in real-time, offering insights that enhance decision-making in business, science, and government.

4. **Enhanced Personalization:** From custom-tailored shopping experiences to adaptive learning in education, AI's ability to learn and predict individual preferences is revolutionizing user experiences.

In a world increasingly driven by data and digital interactions, grasping the basics of AI is not just for tech enthusiasts—it's a vital part of being an informed citizen of the future.

A Sneak Peek at Your Journey Ahead

This book, *Unlocking AI: A Beginner's Guide to the Intelligence of Tomorrow*, is designed to demystify AI. As we progress through the chapters, you'll learn about the building blocks of AI, explore various subfields like machine learning, deep learning, and natural language processing, and see firsthand how AI is applied in everyday scenarios.

Here's a glimpse of what's coming up in the chapters ahead:

- **Understanding the Basics:** We'll start with a simple definition of AI and explore its evolution from early computing concepts to modern applications.

- **How Machines Learn:** Dive into the world of machine learning and discover how algorithms learn from data.

- **Beyond the Algorithms:** Explore AI's creative side, its role in art and music, and even the ethical challenges it poses.

- **Practical Applications:** See how AI is reshaping industries like healthcare, finance, and entertainment, and learn how you can experiment with AI projects yourself.

- **Future Prospects:** Finally, we'll look at emerging trends and consider what the next decade might hold for AI.

Each chapter is crafted to be both informative and engaging, ensuring that you not only learn about AI but also appreciate the wonder and potential behind every innovation.

Embracing the AI Adventure

The world of AI is as exciting as it is transformative. As you turn the pages of this book, you'll discover that AI is not an abstract, inaccessible concept—it's a tool that's already changing the world and one that you can understand, engage with, and even help shape. Whether you're driven by curiosity, professional aspirations, or simply a desire to be prepared for the future, the journey into AI is a rewarding one.

So, let's get started on this adventure. In the coming chapters, we will break down complex ideas into digestible pieces, pepper our discussions with fun examples, and inspire you to see AI as not just a technological advancement but a gateway to new possibilities. Welcome aboard, and prepare to unlock the intelligence of tomorrow!

With that, our journey begins. Turn the page to explore what artificial intelligence really is and how it's poised to revolutionize the way we live, work, and play. Enjoy the ride!

Chapter 2: What is Artificial Intelligence?

Artificial Intelligence, or AI, might sound like a buzzword straight out of a sci-fi movie, but at its core, it represents one of the most transformative fields in modern technology. In this chapter, we'll break down the concept of AI into digestible pieces, exploring its definition, its various branches, and how it manifests in everyday life.

Defining Artificial Intelligence

At its simplest, Artificial Intelligence is the branch of computer science dedicated to creating systems that can perform tasks which would normally require human intelligence. These tasks include understanding language, recognizing patterns, solving problems, and even making decisions. Rather than following a fixed set of instructions, AI systems are designed to learn from data, adapt to new information, and improve over time.

The Two Faces of AI: Narrow vs. General

One of the first distinctions to make when exploring AI is between **narrow (or weak) AI** and **general (or strong) AI**:

- **Narrow AI:**
  This type of AI is designed to perform a specific task or a narrow range of tasks. Examples include voice assistants like Siri and Alexa, recommendation algorithms on streaming services, and image

recognition software used in social media. Narrow AI systems excel in their designated area but don't possess the broader understanding or consciousness that humans do.

- **General AI:**
  Often depicted in science fiction, general AI refers to systems with human-like intelligence. A general AI would be capable of understanding, learning, and applying knowledge across a wide variety of tasks—just as a human can. Despite the excitement it generates, general AI remains a theoretical concept and an ongoing challenge for researchers.

The Building Blocks of AI

Understanding AI means looking under the hood at its core components. Even though AI systems can seem like magic, they are built on fundamental principles that are accessible to anyone willing to dive in.

Data as the New Oil

Data is the lifeblood of AI. Just as a car needs fuel to run, AI systems require vast amounts of data to learn and make decisions. Whether it's images, text, or numerical information, data serves as the raw material from which patterns and insights are extracted. The more quality data an AI has, the better it can learn and perform its tasks.

Algorithms: The Brain of AI

Algorithms are the step-by-step procedures that allow computers to process data and learn from it. In the context of AI, algorithms are often designed to mimic aspects of human thought processes. For example, machine learning algorithms adjust their internal parameters based on the data they're fed, allowing them to improve over time without explicit reprogramming.

The Role of Computing Power

AI's recent leaps in capability have been powered not just by data and smarter algorithms, but also by advances in computing hardware. High-performance GPUs and cloud computing platforms enable AI systems to crunch enormous amounts of data in a fraction of the time that traditional computers would require.

Everyday Examples of AI in Action

Even if you're not an AI expert, you've almost certainly encountered AI in your daily life. Here are a few examples that illustrate how seamlessly AI integrates into our routines:

- **Smartphones:**
  Your phone uses AI to improve photography, optimize battery usage, and even suggest apps or actions based on your habits.

- **Navigation Systems:**
  AI algorithms analyze traffic data in real-time to provide the fastest routes, adjust to unexpected road conditions, and ensure smoother travel.

- **Customer Service:**
  Chatbots powered by AI answer questions, resolve issues, and guide you through processes on websites and apps—often without you even realizing you're interacting with a machine.

- **Streaming Services:**
  Platforms like Netflix and Spotify rely on AI to analyze your viewing or listening history, recommending movies, shows, and songs tailored to your tastes.

These everyday interactions demonstrate that AI is not an abstract concept confined to research labs; it's a practical tool that enhances convenience, efficiency, and personalization in numerous aspects of our lives.

The Broader Spectrum of AI Applications

AI is a broad field, and its applications extend far beyond consumer products. Researchers and professionals are harnessing AI for groundbreaking advancements in various domains:

- **Healthcare:**
  AI systems assist in diagnosing diseases, analyzing medical images, and even predicting patient outcomes. The goal is to support doctors in making faster, more accurate decisions.

- **Finance:**
  In the financial world, AI algorithms help detect fraudulent activities, forecast market trends, and automate trading—all while analyzing vast datasets that would overwhelm human analysts.

- **Education:**
  Personalized learning experiences powered by AI adapt to individual student needs, helping to identify strengths, address weaknesses, and provide targeted educational content.

- **Manufacturing and Logistics:**
  AI optimizes supply chains, improves quality control, and drives the development of autonomous robots capable of performing intricate tasks in challenging environments.

Each of these applications underscores AI's potential to transform industries by enhancing efficiency, accuracy, and overall performance.

Debunking Common Myths

Given its portrayal in movies and popular media, AI is often shrouded in mystery and misunderstanding. Here are a few common myths, along with the realities behind them:

- **Myth:** AI is a conscious, thinking entity.
  Reality: AI systems, including the most advanced ones, are tools built on mathematical models and algorithms. They don't possess emotions, self-awareness, or independent thought.

- **Myth:** AI will inevitably replace all human jobs.
  Reality: While AI can automate certain tasks, it also creates opportunities for new roles and industries. The focus is on augmenting human capabilities rather than outright replacement.

- **Myth:** AI can solve any problem.
  Reality: AI excels in specific tasks, especially those involving pattern recognition and data analysis. However, it often struggles with tasks that require common sense, empathy, or abstract reasoning.

Looking Ahead

Now that we've laid the groundwork by defining AI and exploring its components, you're better equipped to understand the more technical and exciting aspects of this field. As we move forward, we'll delve deeper into specific subfields of AI—like machine learning, deep learning, and natural language processing—providing you with a clearer picture of how these systems work and how they're changing our world.

Artificial Intelligence is a journey of continuous learning and adaptation, much like the systems it creates. In embracing this journey, you're not only gaining technical knowledge but also developing a mindset ready to navigate a rapidly evolving technological landscape.

Welcome to the exploration of AI—a field that's as dynamic as it is transformative. As we turn the page to the next chapter, prepare to dive into the captivating history of AI and witness how ideas that once seemed fantastical are now shaping our everyday reality.

With a solid understanding of what AI is and how it functions at a fundamental level, you're now ready to explore its evolution and the pivotal moments that have brought us to today's technological marvels. Enjoy the journey ahead!

Chapter 3: A Brief History of AI: From Myths to Machines

Artificial Intelligence is not a modern invention—it's the culmination of centuries of human imagination, ingenuity, and technological progress. In this chapter, we'll embark on a historical journey, tracing the evolution of AI from ancient myths and legends to the sophisticated machines of today. By exploring key milestones, fascinating personalities, and pivotal moments, you'll gain an appreciation for how far AI has come and where it might be headed.

From Myth and Legend to Early Dreams

Long before computers ever existed, humans were captivated by the idea of creating beings that could think, learn, and even feel. Ancient myths and legends are filled with tales of artificial beings and mechanical servants:

- **Automata in Antiquity:** Ancient civilizations, from the Greeks to the Chinese, imagined mechanical devices that mimicked human or animal behavior. Stories of self-moving statues and ingenious contraptions hinted at a fascination with replicating life.

- **The Golem of Jewish Folklore:** One of the most enduring legends is that of the golem—a creature fashioned from clay and brought to life through mystical rituals. While the golem was a product of myth, it symbolized humanity's age-old desire to create life from inanimate matter.

- **Renaissance and Beyond:** During the Renaissance, inventors like Leonardo da Vinci sketched designs for mechanical knights and other devices that foreshadowed modern robotics. These early ideas, though limited by the technology of their time, set the stage for future explorations into artificial intelligence.

These early dreams, rooted in mythology and creative storytelling, planted the seeds for a quest that would eventually transform into the scientific field we know today as AI.

The Dawn of Computing: Turing and Early Theories

The 20th century marked a turning point when abstract ideas about machine intelligence began to merge with tangible technological innovations. At the forefront was Alan Turing, a brilliant mathematician whose work laid the groundwork for modern computing and AI.

- **Alan Turing's Vision:** In 1950, Turing published his seminal paper "Computing Machinery and Intelligence," in which he posed the provocative question: "Can machines think?" He introduced what is now known as the Turing Test—a method to evaluate a machine's ability to exhibit human-like intelligence. Turing's ideas challenged the conventional view of machines as mere calculators, suggesting that, with the right programming, they could mimic aspects of human thought.

- **The Concept of a Universal Machine:** Turing's work on the Universal Turing Machine demonstrated that a single machine could, in theory, perform any calculation or process any algorithm, given the appropriate instructions and enough time. This concept is a cornerstone of modern computing and paved the way for the idea that machines could be designed to learn and adapt.

Turing's insights not only advanced the field of computer science but also ignited imaginations, inspiring future generations of researchers to pursue the possibility of machine intelligence.

The Birth of AI as a Field

The formal birth of Artificial Intelligence as an academic discipline is often traced back to the summer of 1956, when a group of researchers gathered at Dartmouth College for what would become known as the Dartmouth Conference.

- **Dartmouth Conference (1956):** Organized by John McCarthy, Marvin Minsky, Nathaniel Rochester, and Claude Shannon, this workshop brought together some of the brightest minds to discuss the potential of machine intelligence. The attendees were optimistic that a machine capable of simulating every aspect of human intelligence was just around the corner.

- **The Optimism of the Early Years:** Early AI researchers made significant strides with rule-based systems, logic programming, and early neural networks. These pioneering efforts laid the foundational concepts of search algorithms, problem-solving methods, and knowledge representation, which continue to underpin modern AI research.

The Dartmouth Conference symbolized a bold new direction for computing—a future where machines could not only calculate but also learn, reason, and perhaps even create.

Milestones and the Evolution of AI

Over the decades, AI research experienced periods of intense progress and frustrating setbacks. Let's explore some of the key milestones that defined its evolution:

The Rise of Expert Systems and Symbolic AI

- **Expert Systems:** In the 1970s and 1980s, researchers developed expert systems designed to emulate the decision-making abilities of human experts. These systems used a collection of rules to solve problems in specific domains such as medical diagnosis or mineral exploration. While expert systems achieved notable successes, they were limited by their reliance on explicit programming and rigid rule structures.

- **Symbolic AI:** Early AI also leaned heavily on symbolic reasoning—manipulating symbols and logical statements to represent knowledge. Although effective in controlled environments, symbolic AI struggled to handle the ambiguity and variability of the real world.

The AI Winters

- **High Hopes and Harsh Realities:** The initial optimism was tempered by periods known as "AI winters," when expectations exceeded practical results. Funding and interest in AI research dwindled during these times, as the limitations of early systems became apparent.

- **Lessons Learned:** These challenging periods, however, were not in vain. They prompted the research community to re-evaluate approaches, leading to more robust methods and a deeper understanding of the complexities involved in creating intelligent systems.

The Resurgence: Machine Learning and Deep Learning

- **The Machine Learning Revolution:** In the 1990s and early 2000s, advances in algorithms, combined with exponentially increasing amounts of data and improved computational power, gave rise to machine learning. Rather than relying solely on pre-programmed rules, machine learning enabled systems to learn patterns directly from data.

- **Deep Learning Breakthroughs:** The advent of deep learning—using neural networks with many layers—ushered in a new era of AI. These models, inspired by the human brain, demonstrated remarkable capabilities in image recognition, speech processing, and natural language understanding. Landmark achievements, such as IBM's Deep Blue defeating world chess champion Garry Kasparov and later Google DeepMind's AlphaGo defeating top human players in the game of Go, captured the world's imagination and solidified AI's potential.

AI Enters the Mainstream

Today, the evolution of AI is not just a tale of academic triumphs and technological breakthroughs—it is a story of transformation that touches every aspect of modern life.

- **Everyday Impact:** From the personalized recommendations on streaming services and e-commerce platforms to the smart assistants in our homes, AI is now woven into the fabric of daily living. Its applications range from mundane tasks to groundbreaking innovations in fields like healthcare, finance, and education.

- **Ongoing Research and Future Prospects:** Despite the impressive progress, the quest for truly human-like intelligence continues. Researchers are exploring new paradigms, such as reinforcement learning, generative models, and hybrid approaches that combine symbolic reasoning with neural networks. The future of AI promises even more seamless integration into our lives, with technologies that adapt, predict, and perhaps even collaborate with us in unprecedented ways.

Reflections on a Dynamic Journey

The history of AI is a vivid tapestry of human creativity, scientific rigor, and the relentless pursuit of understanding intelligence itself. From the mythic golems of ancient lore to the deep neural networks powering today's smart devices, each era has contributed its own unique chapter to the ongoing narrative of artificial intelligence.

- **Innovation Born from Curiosity:** The field of AI has thrived on the human impulse to push boundaries and challenge the status quo. It is a testament to what can be achieved when bold ideas meet technological innovation.

- **The Role of Setbacks:** The periods of disappointment—when lofty expectations met the limitations of existing technology—served as valuable learning experiences. They taught researchers to be patient, to innovate methodically, and to recognize that true breakthroughs often come after overcoming significant obstacles.

- **A Future Unwritten:** As you continue your journey through this book, remember that you are now part of a continuum that stretches from ancient dreams to modern miracles. The evolution of AI is far from complete, and the next chapters will delve into the technologies and ideas that are driving the next wave of innovations.

Conclusion

The story of artificial intelligence is as rich and complex as the human endeavor itself. What began as a series of mythic dreams has evolved into a vibrant field of study that not only redefines technology but also challenges our understanding of intelligence. As we move forward, keep in mind the historical context of AI's development—it offers valuable insights into both the potential and the limitations of the systems we build today.

In the chapters to come, we will dive deeper into the technical aspects of AI, exploring how machines learn, how they interpret the world, and how these capabilities are reshaping industries and societies. With a solid grasp of its history, you're now well-prepared to appreciate the nuances of modern AI and the challenges that lie ahead.

Welcome to the unfolding saga of artificial intelligence—where every breakthrough is a step toward unlocking the intelligence of tomorrow.

Chapter 4: The Building Blocks of AI: Data, Algorithms, and Computing

Artificial Intelligence may seem like magic at times, but behind every intelligent system lies a trio of essential ingredients: data, algorithms, and computing power. In this chapter, we'll break down these fundamental components, explain how they interact, and show you why each one is critical in transforming raw information into intelligent behavior.

Data: The Fuel for Intelligence

Imagine trying to run a car without gasoline. In the world of AI, data plays a similar role—it's the essential fuel that powers every intelligent system.

What Is Data?

Data is any collection of facts, measurements, or observations that can be processed by a computer. In AI, this data can take many forms:

- **Text:** Emails, social media posts, articles, and more.

- **Images:** Photographs, medical scans, satellite imagery.

- **Audio:** Voice recordings, music, ambient sounds.

- **Numbers:** Financial figures, sensor readings, statistical records.

Why Data Matters

1. **Learning Patterns:** AI systems rely on data to learn and identify patterns. For example, by analyzing thousands of cat images, a computer can learn to distinguish cats from other objects.

2. **Training Models:** In machine learning, data is used to train models. The quality and quantity of data directly influence how well an AI system can perform a task.

3. **Real-World Relevance:** Data grounds AI in the real world. The more representative the data, the more accurately an AI system can make decisions that reflect our complex environments.

Data Collection and Preparation

Before data can be used in an AI system, it must often be gathered, cleaned, and organized—a process known as data preprocessing. This includes:

- **Collection:** Aggregating data from various sources (e.g., sensors, databases, online platforms).

- **Cleaning:** Removing errors, duplicates, or irrelevant information.

- **Normalization:** Standardizing data formats to ensure consistency.

- **Labeling:** Annotating data (especially important in

supervised learning) so that the AI knows what each piece of data represents.

Without proper data management, even the most sophisticated algorithms would struggle to produce reliable results.

Algorithms: The Brain Behind the Operation

If data is the fuel, then algorithms are the brains that transform this fuel into intelligent action. An algorithm is a step-by-step set of instructions or rules that a computer follows to solve a problem or perform a task.

The Evolution from Logic to Learning

- **Traditional Algorithms:** Early computer programs used fixed, rule-based algorithms to perform tasks. For example, sorting numbers or executing specific instructions based on conditional statements.

- **Machine Learning Algorithms:** Unlike traditional algorithms, machine learning (ML) algorithms have the ability to learn from data. Instead of being explicitly programmed for every scenario, these algorithms improve their performance over time as they are exposed to more data.

- **Deep Learning and Neural Networks:** Deep learning is a subset of machine learning that employs neural networks—structures inspired by the human brain. These networks consist of layers of interconnected nodes (or neurons) that can process complex data like images, sounds, and language.

How Algorithms Learn

Machine learning algorithms work by adjusting internal parameters to minimize errors when making predictions or decisions. For example:

- **Supervised Learning:** The algorithm is trained on a dataset that includes both the input data and the correct answers (labels). Over time, it learns to map inputs to the correct outputs.

- **Unsupervised Learning:** Here, the algorithm identifies patterns or clusters in data without any predefined labels.

- **Reinforcement Learning:** This approach teaches algorithms through trial and error, rewarding them for making the right decisions and penalizing them for mistakes.

Through these processes, algorithms can develop impressive abilities—from recognizing faces in a crowd to translating languages in real time.

Computing: The Muscle Behind the Magic

Data and algorithms might have the ideas and intelligence, but without computing power, nothing would run at all. Computing refers to the hardware and infrastructure that execute these algorithms and handle massive datasets.

The Role of Computing Power

1. **Processing Speed:** Modern AI tasks often require processing millions of data points in seconds. High-performance processors, especially Graphics Processing Units (GPUs), accelerate these computations far beyond what traditional CPUs can achieve.

2. **Parallel Processing:** Many AI algorithms, particularly those in deep learning, involve calculations that can be done simultaneously. GPUs are designed to handle thousands of such operations in parallel, greatly speeding up the training of complex models.

3. **Scalability:** Cloud computing platforms allow researchers and businesses to access vast amounts of computing power on demand. This scalability is crucial for running large-scale AI projects without investing in expensive hardware upfront.

Hardware Innovations and AI

Over the past decade, advances in computing hardware have been one of the driving forces behind AI breakthroughs. Consider:

- **GPUs and TPUs:** Graphics Processing Units (GPUs) and specialized Tensor Processing Units (TPUs) are engineered to manage the heavy mathematical computations of AI algorithms.

- **Distributed Computing:** Modern AI systems often run on clusters of computers spread across multiple data centers, working together to analyze data and refine models.

- **Edge Computing:** As AI moves into everyday devices, smaller and more efficient computing units are being developed to bring AI processing directly to smartphones, IoT devices, and other gadgets, reducing latency and reliance on centralized data centers.

Bringing It All Together: The AI Ecosystem

The synergy between data, algorithms, and computing power is what brings AI to life. Here's how they work in unison:

- **Data Collection and Processing:** Massive datasets are collected and meticulously prepared, providing the raw material necessary for AI learning.

- **Algorithm Training:** With robust data in hand, machine learning algorithms and neural networks are trained to recognize patterns, make decisions, and even predict future trends.

- **Computational Execution:** All this learning and decision-making happens on powerful computing platforms that perform billions of calculations per second, ensuring that AI systems are both fast and efficient.

This seamless integration creates an ecosystem where each component reinforces the others, enabling technologies like image recognition, natural language processing, and autonomous vehicles to function reliably in the real world.

Conclusion

Understanding the building blocks of AI—data, algorithms, and computing—is essential for grasping how these intelligent systems work and why they're so powerful. Data provides the raw information, algorithms extract meaning and make decisions from that data, and computing power brings everything to life at a scale and speed that would be impossible with human effort alone.

As you continue your journey into the world of AI, keep

these fundamental elements in mind. They form the backbone of not just current AI applications but also the future innovations that will continue to transform our lives. In the next chapters, we'll dive deeper into the fascinating mechanisms of machine learning and explore how these building blocks interact to create systems that can learn, adapt, and even think in ways that mimic human intelligence.

Welcome to the realm where data meets logic and computing turns dreams into reality—this is the heart of artificial intelligence!

Chapter 5: Diving into Machine Learning

Machine learning is at the heart of modern AI. It's the technology that allows computers to learn from data, adapt to new information, and make decisions with minimal human intervention. In this chapter, we'll explore the fundamentals of machine learning in an accessible and engaging way. We'll break down its core concepts, explain how machines learn, and introduce you to the primary methods that power countless applications you encounter every day.

What Is Machine Learning?

At its core, machine learning (ML) is a subset of artificial intelligence that focuses on building systems capable of learning from data rather than following strictly programmed instructions. Instead of explicitly telling a computer what to do in every situation, ML algorithms analyze historical data, identify patterns, and use those patterns to make predictions or decisions when new data comes in.

Imagine teaching a child to recognize animals. Instead of listing every feature of a cat or a dog, you show many pictures of each. Over time, the child begins to understand what distinguishes a cat from a dog. Machine learning works in a similar fashion—by learning from examples.

How Machines Learn

Machine learning involves several key components that work together to transform raw data into actionable intelligence. Here's how the process generally unfolds:

1. **Data Collection:**
   The first step is gathering the right kind of data. This could be images, text, numbers, or any form of information relevant to the task at hand. The quality and quantity of data often determine how well an ML model performs.

2. **Data Preparation:**
   Raw data is rarely perfect. It often needs to be cleaned, organized, and formatted. This process, called preprocessing, might involve removing errors, handling missing values, and converting data into a format that the machine learning algorithm can process effectively.

3. **Choosing an Algorithm:**
   There are many different algorithms in the machine learning toolkit, each suited to specific tasks. The choice of algorithm depends on the nature of the problem and the type of data available. In this chapter, we'll introduce you to the most common approaches: supervised and unsupervised learning.

4. **Training the Model:**

   Training is the process where the algorithm learns from the data. It adjusts its internal parameters by minimizing the difference between its predictions and the actual outcomes. This phase is crucial— much like how repeated practice helps a person improve a skill, training refines the model's ability to make accurate predictions.

5. **Testing and Evaluation:**

   Once the model is trained, it needs to be evaluated on new data that it hasn't seen before. This step helps determine how well the model can generalize its learning to real-world scenarios. Evaluation metrics might include accuracy, precision, recall, or other domain-specific measures.

6. **Deployment and Improvement:**

   After testing, the model is deployed to perform real tasks, such as filtering spam emails or recommending movies. As more data is collected, the model can be retrained and improved, continuously evolving to become more effective over time.

Supervised Learning: Learning With Guidance

Supervised learning is like learning with a teacher. In this approach, the model is trained on a labeled dataset, meaning each example in the training data is paired with the correct answer or outcome.

How It Works

- **Input and Output:**
  The model receives input data along with the corresponding correct output. For example, imagine a dataset of emails labeled as "spam" or "not spam." The algorithm learns to associate certain features (like specific words or phrases) with each label.

- **Learning Process:**
  During training, the model makes predictions and then adjusts its parameters based on the difference between its predictions and the actual labels. Over time, it gets better at mapping inputs to the correct outputs.

- **Real-World Examples:**

  - **Email Filtering:** Identifying spam emails based on characteristics learned from labeled examples.

  - **Image Recognition:** Classifying pictures as cats, dogs, or other objects after being trained on thousands of labeled images.

  - **Medical Diagnosis:** Helping doctors diagnose diseases by analyzing patient data that has been previously labeled with known conditions.

Supervised learning is one of the most widely used machine learning techniques due to its effectiveness in tasks where historical labeled data is available.

Unsupervised Learning: Discovering Hidden Patterns

Unsupervised learning is more like exploration without a map. In this method, the model is given data without any labels and must find patterns or structures on its own.

How It Works

- **Finding Patterns:**
  The algorithm examines the data and looks for similarities, differences, clusters, or other underlying structures. Without guidance, it identifies inherent groupings in the data.

- **Techniques and Applications:**

  o **Clustering:** Grouping similar data points together. For instance, a retailer might use clustering to segment customers based on buying habits.

  o **Dimensionality Reduction:** Simplifying data by reducing the number of features, which helps in visualizing complex datasets or speeding up other algorithms.

- ○ **Anomaly Detection:** Identifying unusual data points that don't fit the normal pattern, which can be useful for fraud detection or quality control.

Unsupervised learning is particularly valuable when you have large amounts of unlabeled data and need to uncover hidden relationships or structures that aren't immediately obvious.

A Glimpse at Other Learning Paradigms

While supervised and unsupervised learning are the two most common approaches, there are other methods as well:

- **Reinforcement Learning:**
  In reinforcement learning, an agent learns by interacting with its environment. It receives rewards or penalties based on its actions, gradually discovering strategies that maximize rewards. This approach is popular in fields such as robotics and game playing.

- **Semi-Supervised Learning:**
  Sometimes, a dataset may contain a small amount of labeled data alongside a larger pool of unlabeled data. Semi-supervised learning techniques

leverage both to improve learning accuracy without the need for extensive labeling efforts.

Each of these paradigms offers different strengths and is suited to different types of problems. As you advance in your journey, you might explore these methods in more depth.

Real-World Example: Teaching a Computer to Recognize Handwritten Digits

One of the classic examples used to illustrate machine learning is the task of recognizing handwritten digits, such as those in the MNIST dataset. Here's a simplified version of how it works:

1. **Data Collection:**
   Thousands of images of handwritten digits (0 through 9) are collected, with each image labeled with the correct digit.

2. **Training the Model:**
   A supervised learning algorithm is used to train a model on this dataset. The model examines the pixel patterns in each image and learns to associate these patterns with the correct number.

3. **Testing:**
   Once trained, the model is tested on new images it hasn't seen before. If it can accurately identify the

digits in these new images, the model is considered successful.

4. **Application:**

   This same approach can be extended to more complex tasks like recognizing objects in photographs or processing handwritten text in various languages.

This example illustrates how machine learning takes a complex, variable task and breaks it down into a process of learning from examples, ultimately leading to reliable performance in real-world applications.

The Impact and Future of Machine Learning

Machine learning is transforming industries and revolutionizing how we interact with technology. From personalized recommendations on streaming platforms to self-driving cars that learn from vast amounts of road data, ML is at the core of many innovations.

As computational power continues to grow and more data becomes available, machine learning models are expected to become even more accurate and versatile. Researchers are constantly exploring new techniques and algorithms that push the boundaries of what machines can learn and achieve.

Moreover, as machine learning becomes more integrated

into our daily lives, ethical considerations—such as fairness, privacy, and transparency—are taking center stage. It's essential to understand not only how these systems work but also the responsibilities that come with deploying them.

Conclusion

Machine learning is a dynamic and rapidly evolving field that brings us closer to creating systems capable of intelligent behavior. By learning from data, these models can solve complex problems, adapt to new situations, and provide insights that would be difficult for humans to uncover on their own.

In this chapter, we've covered the fundamental principles of machine learning, explored the differences between supervised and unsupervised learning, and looked at real-world examples that illustrate how machines learn. As you continue your journey into the world of AI, keep in mind that machine learning is not just a technological tool—it's a gateway to understanding and harnessing the potential of intelligent systems.

In the chapters ahead, we will delve deeper into specialized areas of AI, including deep learning, natural language processing, and more. For now, let this chapter serve as your introduction to the fascinating process by which machines learn, adapt, and help shape the future of technology.

Welcome to the adventure of machine learning—where data, algorithms, and a little bit of magic combine to create a smarter tomorrow!

Chapter 6: Deep Learning Demystified

Deep learning is often portrayed as the magic behind many of today's AI breakthroughs—from self-driving cars to voice assistants that understand your every command. In this chapter, we'll explore the fascinating world of deep learning, breaking down its core concepts and showing you how these systems learn and process complex information. We'll demystify the jargon and technicalities to reveal how deep learning brings intelligence closer to human capabilities.

What Is Deep Learning?

Deep learning is a specialized subfield of machine learning that uses structures known as neural networks—networks of interconnected nodes, or "neurons"—to process data and make decisions. Inspired by the architecture of the human brain, these networks are organized into layers, which allow them to learn multiple levels of abstraction.

Key Characteristics

- **Layered Architecture:**
  Unlike simpler machine learning models, deep learning models consist of many layers (sometimes dozens or even hundreds). Each layer processes input from the previous layer and passes its output to the next, gradually extracting higher-level

features.

- **Neural Networks:**
  The backbone of deep learning is the artificial neural network. Each neuron in these networks takes input data, processes it through a mathematical function, and passes it on. Together, they form a web that can learn to recognize patterns, from edges in an image to the sentiment behind a sentence.

- **Learning Complex Representations:**
  Deep learning models excel at automatically discovering representations and features from raw data. For instance, in image recognition, early layers might learn to detect simple shapes and colors, while deeper layers identify more abstract concepts like faces or objects.

Understanding Neural Networks

At the heart of deep learning lies the neural network. Let's break down its key components and how they work together:

1. Neurons and Layers

- **Neurons:**
  Think of a neuron as a tiny decision-maker. Each neuron receives inputs (which can be raw data or

outputs from previous neurons), multiplies them by weights (which determine the importance of each input), adds a bias, and then passes the result through an activation function. This function introduces non-linearity, allowing the network to learn complex relationships.

- **Layers:**
  Neural networks are organized into layers:

    o **Input Layer:** Receives the raw data (such as pixel values from an image).

    o **Hidden Layers:** These are the intermediate layers where most of the processing happens. A network with many hidden layers is known as a deep neural network.

    o **Output Layer:** Produces the final prediction or classification result.

2. The Learning Process: Forward Propagation and Backpropagation

- **Forward Propagation:**
  During the forward pass, data moves through the network from the input layer to the output layer. At each neuron, the weighted inputs are summed, an activation function is applied, and the output is passed to the next layer. This process culminates in the final output of the model.

- **Backpropagation:**
Once the output is generated, the network needs to learn from its errors. Backpropagation is the method by which the network adjusts its weights. It works by:

  1. Calculating the error between the predicted output and the actual result.

  2. Propagating this error backward through the network.

  3. Adjusting the weights to minimize the error.

This iterative process continues until the network's predictions improve significantly.

Deep Learning in Action: Applications and Examples

Deep learning's power lies in its versatility and its ability to work with large, unstructured datasets. Here are some real-world applications:

Image Recognition

- **Facial Recognition:**
Deep learning models are widely used in security systems and smartphones to recognize and verify human faces.

- **Medical Imaging:**
In healthcare, deep learning helps radiologists

detect anomalies in X-rays, MRIs, and CT scans, often spotting issues earlier than traditional methods.

Natural Language Processing (NLP)

- **Voice Assistants:**
  Systems like Siri, Alexa, and Google Assistant use deep learning to understand and respond to spoken commands.

- **Language Translation:**
  Deep learning models power translation services, enabling them to convert text between languages with remarkable accuracy.

Autonomous Vehicles

- **Self-Driving Cars:**
  Deep learning algorithms process data from cameras, radar, and lidar sensors to identify road signs, pedestrians, and other vehicles, enabling safe navigation.

Game Playing and Decision Making

- **AlphaGo:**
  Deep learning was central to Google DeepMind's AlphaGo, which famously defeated world champions in the game of Go by evaluating countless possible moves and strategies.

Advantages and Challenges

Advantages

- **Automatic Feature Extraction:**
  One of the greatest strengths of deep learning is its ability to automatically identify and extract important features from raw data without human intervention.

- **Handling Complex Data:**
  Deep learning excels in processing unstructured data such as images, audio, and text—areas where traditional machine learning methods might struggle.

- **Scalability:**
  With the explosion of available data and powerful computing resources, deep learning models can be trained on massive datasets, further enhancing their performance.

Challenges

- **Data Requirements:**
  Deep learning models typically require vast amounts of data to achieve high accuracy, which can be a limitation in data-scarce domains.

- **Computational Demands:**
  Training deep networks is resource-intensive, often requiring specialized hardware like GPUs or TPUs

and considerable time.

- **Interpretability:**
Deep learning models are often described as "black boxes" because it can be difficult to understand exactly how they arrive at their decisions. This lack of transparency can be problematic in critical applications where explainability is crucial.

The Future of Deep Learning

Deep learning is a rapidly evolving field with exciting prospects on the horizon. Researchers are continually developing more efficient architectures and training methods to overcome current challenges. Some emerging trends include:

- **Transfer Learning:**
This approach allows a pre-trained model to be fine-tuned for a new task with relatively little additional data, making deep learning more accessible in specialized domains.

- **Generative Models:**
Models like Generative Adversarial Networks (GANs) are pushing the boundaries of what AI can create, from realistic images to entirely new pieces of music or art.

- **Hybrid Approaches:**
  Combining deep learning with other techniques, such as symbolic reasoning or reinforcement learning, is an active area of research that may lead to more robust and adaptable AI systems.

As deep learning continues to evolve, its influence will expand into even more areas of our lives, offering new ways to solve problems and unlock creativity.

Conclusion

Deep learning represents one of the most exciting frontiers in AI—a field that continuously pushes the boundaries of what machines can do. By mimicking the structure and function of the human brain, deep neural networks have transformed our ability to process and interpret complex data. Whether it's recognizing a friend's face in a crowd or powering the next generation of autonomous vehicles, deep learning is at the core of these advancements.

In this chapter, we demystified deep learning by exploring its fundamental components, the mechanics of neural networks, and real-world applications that are changing our world. As you move forward in your journey through AI, keep in mind that while deep learning is powerful, it is also just one piece of a larger puzzle—a puzzle that continues to expand with each new discovery.

Welcome to the deep end of AI—where every layer of understanding brings you closer to unlocking the intelligence of tomorrow!

Chapter 7: Natural Language Processing: Teaching Machines to Understand Us

Language is one of humanity's most powerful tools, and for decades, researchers have strived to teach machines to understand, interpret, and even generate human language. Natural Language Processing (NLP) is the field of AI dedicated to bridging the communication gap between humans and computers. In this chapter, we'll explore how NLP works, the challenges it faces, and the transformative impact it has on our daily lives.

Introduction: The Quest for Language Understanding

Imagine being able to talk to your computer or phone just as you would to a friend, and have it understand your words, tone, and even the context behind them. This is the promise of Natural Language Processing. From the early days of simple command-line interfaces to today's sophisticated virtual assistants like Siri, Alexa, and Google Assistant, NLP has evolved significantly. The ability for machines to grasp the nuances of human language not only makes technology more accessible but also revolutionizes how we interact with the digital world.

The Evolution of NLP

Early Beginnings

The journey of NLP began with rule-based systems that relied on handcrafted grammars and dictionaries. Early applications were simple and limited—think of spell checkers or basic text search algorithms—but they laid the groundwork for more advanced systems. Researchers initially focused on syntactic analysis, breaking down sentences into parts of speech, and developing formal grammars that could model language structure.

The Statistical Turn

The limitations of rule-based approaches soon became apparent. Language is inherently ambiguous and complex, making it nearly impossible to capture all its nuances with static rules. The introduction of statistical methods in the 1990s marked a significant turning point. By leveraging large corpora of text, researchers began using probabilistic models to predict language patterns. Techniques like n-grams and Hidden Markov Models (HMMs) allowed computers to model language more flexibly by calculating the likelihood of word sequences.

The Deep Learning Revolution

In recent years, deep learning has transformed NLP. Neural networks, particularly recurrent neural networks (RNNs) and later, transformer models like BERT and GPT, have achieved unprecedented success in understanding and generating human language. These models can learn context and subtle nuances from vast datasets, leading to breakthroughs in tasks like machine translation, text summarization, and sentiment analysis.

Core Concepts in NLP

To appreciate the intricacies of NLP, it's essential to understand its key components and tasks:

1. Tokenization

Tokenization is the process of breaking text down into smaller pieces, or tokens. These tokens can be words, phrases, or even individual characters. Tokenization is the first step in NLP, as it converts raw text into a format that can be analyzed. For example, the sentence "Hello, world!" might be tokenized into "Hello", ",", and "world".

2. Parsing and Syntactic Analysis

Parsing involves analyzing the grammatical structure of a sentence. Syntactic analysis identifies parts of speech (nouns, verbs, adjectives, etc.) and maps out the relationships between them. This helps in understanding how words function together to convey meaning. Techniques such as dependency parsing and constituency parsing are commonly used in this stage.

3. Semantic Analysis

While syntax deals with structure, semantics is all about meaning. Semantic analysis aims to understand the meaning behind words and phrases. This can involve:

- **Word Sense Disambiguation:** Determining which meaning of a word is used in a given context.

- **Named Entity Recognition (NER):** Identifying proper names like people, organizations, or locations within the text.

- **Sentiment Analysis:** Assessing the emotional tone behind a body of text—whether it is positive, negative, or neutral.

4. Context and Pragmatics

Understanding language goes beyond just the literal meaning of words. Context and pragmatics consider factors like tone, sarcasm, idioms, and cultural references. Advanced NLP systems incorporate context by considering surrounding words (contextual embeddings) and even the broader conversation to interpret meaning more accurately.

Techniques and Algorithms in NLP

Modern NLP employs a variety of techniques, each suited to different types of tasks and challenges:

Statistical Methods

Before the advent of deep learning, statistical methods dominated NLP. These methods rely on probability and large datasets to make predictions. For instance, n-gram models estimate the probability of a word based on the preceding words, which can be used in applications like predictive text.

Machine Learning Approaches

Traditional machine learning methods, such as Support Vector Machines (SVMs) and decision trees, have been used for text classification tasks, such as spam detection and sentiment analysis. These models often require careful feature engineering—extracting meaningful attributes from text to feed into the algorithm.

Deep Learning and Neural Networks

Deep learning has brought a paradigm shift in NLP with models that automatically learn features from raw text data:

- **Recurrent Neural Networks (RNNs):** Designed to handle sequences, RNNs maintain information about previous inputs, which makes them well-suited for language tasks.

- **Long Short-Term Memory Networks (LSTMs):** A type of RNN that overcomes the short-term memory limitations of basic RNNs, enabling better handling of long sentences and paragraphs.

- **Transformers:** Models like BERT, GPT, and their successors have revolutionized NLP by using self-attention mechanisms to weigh the importance of different words in a sentence. These models can capture context more effectively than their predecessors and are currently the state-of-the-art in many NLP tasks.

Transfer Learning in NLP

Transfer learning involves pre-training a model on a large dataset and then fine-tuning it on a specific task. This approach has significantly reduced the amount of data and time required to train effective NLP models. Pre-trained models such as BERT or GPT-3 can be adapted for tasks ranging from translation to question answering, making them incredibly versatile.

Real-World Applications of NLP

The practical applications of NLP are as varied as they are impactful. Here are a few examples that illustrate its transformative power:

Virtual Assistants and Chatbots

Virtual assistants like Siri, Alexa, and Google Assistant use NLP to understand voice commands, interpret user intent, and generate appropriate responses. Chatbots on customer service websites similarly leverage NLP to handle inquiries, resolve issues, and improve user experience without human intervention.

Machine Translation

Services like Google Translate and DeepL utilize NLP to convert text from one language to another. Modern translation systems can grasp context, idiomatic expressions, and cultural nuances, providing translations that are both accurate and natural-sounding.

Sentiment Analysis

Businesses use sentiment analysis to monitor public opinion on social media, reviews, and forums. By analyzing the language used by consumers, companies can gauge the emotional response to products, services, or marketing campaigns, enabling more informed strategic decisions.

Information Extraction and Summarization

NLP is essential for sifting through massive amounts of unstructured text to extract key information. This includes summarizing lengthy articles, generating reports, and even assisting in legal and medical document analysis by identifying relevant sections and entities.

Content Generation

Recent advances in NLP have led to the creation of models capable of generating human-like text. From drafting emails and writing articles to composing poetry and creative stories, these generative models are pushing the boundaries of what machines can create.

Challenges in Natural Language Processing

Despite its many successes, NLP faces several ongoing challenges:

Ambiguity and Variability

Human language is inherently ambiguous. A single word can have multiple meanings depending on context, and the same idea can be expressed in countless ways. This variability makes it difficult for NLP systems to achieve perfect understanding.

Contextual Nuances

Understanding the full context of a conversation—such as sarcasm, humor, or cultural references—remains a significant hurdle. While transformer models have improved context handling, capturing the subtleties of human communication is still an evolving area of research.

Data Bias and Ethical Considerations

NLP models learn from the data they are trained on, which can contain biases present in society. This can lead to models that inadvertently reinforce stereotypes or make unfair decisions. Addressing these biases and ensuring ethical use of NLP is a critical concern for researchers and developers.

Multilingual and Low-Resource Languages

While NLP has made impressive strides in widely spoken languages like English, challenges remain for languages with fewer digital resources. Developing effective models for low-resource languages requires creative solutions to data scarcity and cultural nuances.

The Future of NLP

The future of NLP is both exciting and full of promise. As research continues, we can expect:

- **More Context-Aware Systems:** Models that understand not just words, but the intent, emotion, and context behind them.

- **Improved Multilingual Capabilities:** Broader support for languages around the world, making technology more inclusive and globally accessible.

- **Ethical and Transparent AI:** Enhanced focus on developing systems that are not only powerful but also fair, unbiased, and explainable.

- **Integration Across Domains:** Deeper integration of NLP with other fields such as robotics, augmented reality, and healthcare, leading to innovative applications that enhance our interaction with technology.

Conclusion

Natural Language Processing is the cornerstone of making technology more human-centric. By teaching machines to understand our language, NLP bridges the gap between human thought and digital communication. In this chapter, we've explored the evolution of NLP, its core concepts, the techniques that drive it, and the remarkable real-world applications that are changing the way we interact with the world.

As you continue your journey into the realm of artificial intelligence, keep in mind that NLP is not just about translating words—it's about capturing the essence of human communication. With each advancement, we move closer to a future where our devices not only respond to commands but truly understand our needs and intentions.

Welcome to the world of language and intelligence—where every word brings us closer to unlocking the full potential of human-machine interaction!

Chapter 8: Computer Vision: How Machines See and Interpret the World

Computer vision is the technology that empowers machines to interpret and make decisions based on visual data. From facial recognition on smartphones to autonomous vehicles navigating busy streets, computer vision has become a cornerstone of modern technology. In this chapter, we'll explore the fundamentals of computer vision, discuss its evolution, and examine how algorithms and neural networks enable machines to "see" the world around us.

What Is Computer Vision?

At its essence, computer vision is a field of artificial intelligence that trains computers to interpret and understand the visual world. By processing and analyzing digital images and videos, computer vision systems can identify objects, classify scenes, and even detect subtle patterns that might be invisible to the human eye.

Core Objectives

- **Recognition:** Identifying objects, people, or specific features within an image.

- **Detection:** Locating instances of objects or regions of interest.

- **Segmentation:** Dividing an image into parts for

easier analysis.

- **Tracking:** Following objects over time in video streams.

- **Interpretation:** Understanding complex scenes to derive actionable insights.

By mimicking the human visual system, computer vision aims to automate tasks that have traditionally required human interpretation, thereby increasing speed, accuracy, and efficiency in a range of applications.

The Evolution of Computer Vision

The journey of computer vision mirrors the broader evolution of AI—from rule-based systems to advanced deep learning models.

Early Days: Handcrafted Features and Classical Methods

- **Traditional Image Processing:** In its early stages, computer vision relied on handcrafted algorithms and feature detectors such as edge detection (e.g., the Sobel or Canny operators) and corner detection. These methods helped to extract basic geometric features from images.

- **Template Matching:** Early applications often used template matching techniques where predefined patterns were compared against portions of an image to find a match. Although simple, this approach was limited by its inflexibility in dealing with variations in scale, rotation, or lighting.

The Rise of Machine Learning

As computational power increased, machine learning techniques began to influence computer vision:

- **Feature Extraction:** Algorithms such as Scale-Invariant Feature Transform (SIFT) and Speeded-Up Robust Features (SURF) automated the process of identifying key points in an image, enabling more robust matching and recognition.

- **Statistical Models:** Early machine learning models, such as Support Vector Machines (SVMs), were used in conjunction with these features to classify images and detect objects.

The Deep Learning Revolution

The advent of deep learning transformed computer vision by eliminating the need for manual feature extraction:

- **Convolutional Neural Networks (CNNs):** CNNs, with their ability to automatically learn hierarchical features from raw image data, have dramatically improved the accuracy of image classification, object detection, and segmentation tasks. Landmark models such as AlexNet, VGGNet, and ResNet have set new performance standards on benchmark datasets.

- **End-to-End Learning:** Modern deep learning models can process raw pixels and directly output decisions or predictions, streamlining the pipeline and making systems more robust to variations in input data.

Key Concepts in Computer Vision

Understanding computer vision involves grasping several key concepts that form the backbone of how machines process visual information.

Image Representation

- **Pixels and Color Channels:** Digital images are made up of pixels, where each pixel contains color information typically represented in RGB (red, green, blue) channels. Other color spaces like HSV or grayscale are also used depending on the application.

- **Resolution and Scale:** The level of detail in an image depends on its resolution. High-resolution images provide more detail but require more processing power, while lower-resolution images can be processed faster.

Feature Extraction and Representation

- **Edges and Textures:** Early vision algorithms focused on detecting edges, which are significant transitions in pixel intensity. Texture analysis also plays a crucial role in identifying patterns.

- **Descriptors:** Methods like SIFT and SURF generate descriptors that encode local image information, making it possible to compare and match features across images.

Object Recognition and Localization

- **Classification:** This process involves assigning a label to an image or a region within it. Deep learning has excelled at classifying objects with high accuracy.

- **Detection:** Object detection not only identifies what is in an image but also where it is located. Techniques such as the Region-based CNN (R-CNN) family, YOLO (You Only Look Once), and SSD (Single Shot MultiBox Detector) have advanced this field significantly.

- **Segmentation:** Image segmentation divides an image into meaningful parts. Semantic segmentation assigns a class to every pixel, while instance segmentation distinguishes between individual objects of the same class.

Techniques and Algorithms in Computer Vision

Computer vision employs a variety of techniques that have evolved over the years. Here are some of the most significant methods:

Traditional Algorithms

- **Edge Detection:** Algorithms such as the Canny edge detector highlight the boundaries within an image.

- **Haar Cascades:** Used for object detection, these classifiers quickly identify features like faces in images.

- **Optical Flow:** This technique tracks the motion of objects between frames in a video, which is essential for video analysis and motion estimation.

Deep Learning Approaches

- **Convolutional Neural Networks (CNNs):** CNNs have become the workhorse of computer vision. They are particularly effective for tasks like image classification and object detection.

- **Recurrent Neural Networks (RNNs) in Video Analysis:** For video processing, RNNs and Long Short-Term Memory Networks (LSTMs) help model temporal dependencies across frames.

- **Generative Models:** Techniques such as Generative Adversarial Networks (GANs) can create realistic images and have applications in image synthesis, enhancement, and data augmentation.

Hybrid Methods

- **Feature Pyramid Networks (FPNs):** These networks combine features at multiple scales, enhancing the ability to detect objects of varying sizes.

- **Attention Mechanisms:** Borrowed from NLP, attention mechanisms help focus the model on important regions within an image, leading to improved performance in complex scenes.

Real-World Applications of Computer Vision

The practical applications of computer vision are extensive and touch many aspects of modern life:

Autonomous Vehicles

- **Navigation and Safety:** Self-driving cars rely on computer vision to detect road signs, pedestrians, other vehicles, and obstacles. Real-time processing of visual data is critical for making safe driving decisions.

- **Lane Detection and Traffic Analysis:** Algorithms track lane markings and monitor traffic conditions to assist with navigation and adaptive driving strategies.

Healthcare

- **Medical Imaging:** Computer vision assists radiologists by identifying abnormalities in X-rays, MRIs, and CT scans. Automated analysis can help in early diagnosis of diseases such as cancer.

- **Surgical Assistance:** Real-time image analysis during surgery can help guide robotic instruments and improve surgical outcomes.

Security and Surveillance

- **Facial Recognition:** Used in both public security systems and personal devices, facial recognition algorithms can identify individuals in crowded places.

- **Behavior Analysis:** Surveillance systems employ computer vision to detect unusual behavior, aiding in the prevention of crime and enhancing public safety.

Retail and Customer Experience

- **Inventory Management:** Computer vision systems can track products on shelves, manage stock levels, and detect when items need restocking.

- **Augmented Reality (AR):** AR applications use computer vision to overlay digital information on the real world, enhancing shopping experiences and interactive advertising.

Challenges in Computer Vision

Despite its rapid progress, computer vision faces several challenges:

Variability in Visual Data

- **Lighting and Weather Conditions:** Changes in illumination, shadows, and weather can significantly affect the quality of visual data, making it challenging for algorithms to maintain accuracy.

- **Occlusions and Clutter:** Objects in real-world scenes are often partially obscured or surrounded by irrelevant details, complicating detection and recognition.

Scalability and Computational Demands

- **Processing High-Resolution Images:** High-resolution images require significant computational power and memory, which can limit real-time applications.

- **Data Requirements:** Training deep learning models typically demands large datasets with diverse examples to generalize effectively across different scenarios.

Bias and Fairness

- **Data Imbalance:** If training datasets are not diverse, models may develop biases that affect performance across different demographics or environments.

- **Interpretability:** Like many deep learning systems, computer vision models can be opaque, making it difficult to understand how decisions are made—a concern in critical applications such as law enforcement or healthcare.

The Future of Computer Vision

Looking ahead, the field of computer vision is poised for further innovation and integration into everyday technology:

- **Edge Computing:** As hardware becomes more powerful and efficient, computer vision algorithms will increasingly run on edge devices, reducing latency and enabling real-time processing in applications like augmented reality.

- **Improved Models:** Advances in neural network architectures and training techniques will continue to improve the accuracy, speed, and robustness of computer vision systems.

- **Cross-Modal Integration:** The combination of computer vision with other AI fields—such as natural language processing—will lead to more holistic systems that can interpret both visual and textual information, enhancing applications in robotics and human-computer interaction.

- **Ethical and Transparent AI:** Ongoing research into model interpretability and fairness will help ensure that computer vision systems are not only powerful but also equitable and trustworthy.

Conclusion

Computer vision stands as one of the most dynamic and transformative areas of artificial intelligence. By enabling machines to interpret and understand visual data, it has unlocked countless applications—from autonomous vehicles and healthcare to security and retail. In this chapter, we explored the core concepts, techniques, and challenges of computer vision, as well as its evolution from early handcrafted methods to modern deep learning models.

As we continue to integrate computer vision into our daily lives, its potential to transform industries and enhance human experiences is boundless. The journey of teaching machines to see and interpret the world is ongoing, promising a future where technology not only reacts to visual information but understands it in increasingly sophisticated ways.

Welcome to the visionary realm of computer vision—where every pixel tells a story, and every image opens a new window into the intelligence of tomorrow!

Chapter 9: Reinforcement Learning: Learning Through Rewards and Punishments

Imagine teaching a dog new tricks by offering treats when it behaves correctly and withholding rewards when it doesn't. Reinforcement learning (RL) operates on a similar principle, allowing machines to learn through trial and error. In this chapter, we'll explore the fascinating world of reinforcement learning, unpack its core concepts, and examine how it empowers machines to make decisions and improve through feedback. From fundamental theories to real-world applications, this chapter will guide you through the exciting process of learning by rewards and punishments.

What Is Reinforcement Learning?

Reinforcement learning is a branch of machine learning where an agent learns to make decisions by interacting with its environment. Unlike supervised learning, where models learn from a dataset with known answers, or unsupervised learning, where the focus is on finding hidden patterns, RL emphasizes learning from the consequences of actions. The agent receives feedback in the form of rewards or penalties, using this information to shape its future behavior.

Key Components

- **Agent:** The learner or decision-maker that interacts with the environment.

- **Environment:** Everything the agent interacts with—the world in which it operates.

- **State:** A representation of the current situation or context the agent is in.

- **Action:** Any move or decision the agent makes that can change its state.

- **Reward:** Feedback received from the environment after an action, indicating the success or failure of that action.

- **Policy:** The strategy that the agent uses to decide on actions based on the current state.

- **Value Function:** A measure of the long-term benefit of states or actions, guiding the agent to achieve maximum cumulative rewards.

Reinforcement learning can be thought of as a loop: the agent observes its state, takes an action, receives a reward, and updates its policy—all in an ongoing cycle aimed at maximizing long-term benefits.

The Learning Process: From Exploration to Exploitation

At the heart of reinforcement learning lies the balance between two competing strategies: exploration and exploitation.

Exploration vs. Exploitation

- **Exploration:** Involves trying out new actions to discover their potential rewards. This is essential for learning about the environment and understanding which actions yield the best outcomes.

- **Exploitation:** Focuses on leveraging known actions that have previously resulted in high rewards to maximize benefits.

Striking the right balance is crucial. An agent that explores too much may waste time on suboptimal actions, while an agent that exploits too heavily might miss out on better strategies it hasn't yet discovered.

Learning Algorithms

Several key algorithms have been developed to facilitate reinforcement learning, each with its unique approach to managing this balance:

- **Q-Learning:**
  One of the simplest yet most powerful algorithms, Q-learning uses a Q-table to estimate the value (expected cumulative reward) of taking a particular

action in a given state. The agent updates this table as it gathers experience, eventually learning an optimal policy without needing a model of the environment.

- **SARSA (State-Action-Reward-State-Action):**
Similar to Q-learning but with a key difference: SARSA updates its Q-values based on the action actually taken in the next state, rather than the best possible action. This approach makes SARSA more conservative and sensitive to the agent's current policy.

- **Policy Gradient Methods:**
Instead of learning value functions, policy gradient methods directly optimize the policy. These methods are particularly useful in high-dimensional or continuous action spaces, where traditional value-based methods may struggle.

- **Actor-Critic Models:**
Combining the strengths of both value-based and policy-based methods, actor-critic models have two components: the actor, which decides on actions, and the critic, which evaluates them. This division allows the agent to benefit from both direct policy optimization and value estimation.

Real-World Applications

Reinforcement learning has found its way into a variety of exciting and practical applications:

Gaming and Simulation

- **Game Playing:**
  RL has achieved remarkable successes in games. Notably, DeepMind's AlphaGo used reinforcement learning to defeat world champions in the complex game of Go by learning strategies through countless simulated matches.

- **Video Games:**
  RL is used to train non-player characters (NPCs) in video games, enabling them to adapt to players' actions and provide a more challenging and engaging experience.

Robotics and Autonomous Systems

- **Robotic Control:**
  In robotics, reinforcement learning helps develop control policies for tasks like grasping objects, walking, or navigating unfamiliar terrains. Robots learn to adjust their movements based on trial and error, improving their performance over time.

- **Autonomous Vehicles:**
  Self-driving cars employ RL to make real-time decisions such as lane changes, obstacle avoidance,

and route optimization. By continuously interacting with their environment, these systems learn to navigate safely under diverse conditions.

Industrial and Financial Applications

- **Optimization and Scheduling:**
  Reinforcement learning is used to optimize complex processes like supply chain management, energy distribution, and manufacturing scheduling, where the goal is to maximize efficiency and minimize costs.

- **Algorithmic Trading:**
  In finance, RL algorithms help develop trading strategies that adjust to market dynamics, learning from the successes and failures of past trades to improve future performance.

Advantages and Challenges of Reinforcement Learning

Advantages

- **Autonomous Learning:**
  RL agents learn from direct interaction with their environment, enabling them to discover effective strategies without explicit instructions.

- **Adaptability:**
  Because reinforcement learning is based on

continuous feedback, agents can adapt to changing environments and learn from new experiences.

- **Broad Applicability:**
  RL is versatile, with applications ranging from robotics and gaming to finance and industrial optimization.

Challenges

- **Sample Efficiency:**
  RL often requires a large number of interactions with the environment to learn an effective policy, which can be computationally expensive and time-consuming.

- **Reward Design:**
  Crafting an appropriate reward function is critical yet challenging. Poorly designed rewards can lead to unintended behaviors or suboptimal learning outcomes.

- **Exploration vs. Exploitation Dilemma:**
  Striking the right balance between exploring new strategies and exploiting known rewards is an ongoing challenge in RL research.

- **Stability and Convergence:**
  Training RL models, especially in complex environments, can be unstable and may not always converge to the optimal policy.

The Future of Reinforcement Learning

Reinforcement learning is a rapidly evolving field with a bright future. Researchers are actively developing new methods to improve sample efficiency, stability, and scalability. Some promising areas of exploration include:

- **Model-Based Reinforcement Learning:**
  By incorporating models of the environment, agents can simulate interactions and plan actions more effectively, reducing the need for extensive real-world experimentation.

- **Hierarchical Reinforcement Learning:**
  Breaking down complex tasks into simpler sub-tasks, hierarchical RL allows agents to learn at multiple levels of abstraction, enhancing performance on sophisticated tasks.

- **Multi-Agent Systems:**
  As RL expands into scenarios with multiple interacting agents, techniques are being developed to manage collaboration and competition, leading to more robust and dynamic systems.

The advances in these areas are poised to unlock even more powerful applications of reinforcement learning, pushing the boundaries of what intelligent machines can achieve.

Conclusion

Reinforcement learning offers a dynamic and intuitive approach to machine learning by mimicking the natural process of learning from rewards and punishments. Through the interaction of agents with their environment, RL enables systems to adapt, improve, and develop strategies that maximize long-term rewards. In this chapter, we've explored the fundamental principles of reinforcement learning, delved into its key algorithms, and examined real-world applications that demonstrate its transformative potential.

As you continue your journey into the world of artificial intelligence, keep in mind that reinforcement learning not only equips machines to make decisions but also challenges us to think critically about learning, adaptation, and the nature of intelligence itself. Embracing the trial-and-error process, RL paves the way for smarter, more autonomous systems that are set to redefine our interaction with technology.

Welcome to the world of learning through rewards and punishments—a realm where every action counts and every mistake is a stepping stone to a brighter, more intelligent future!

Chapter 10: The Math Behind AI: A Beginner's Crash Course

Mathematics is often seen as the hidden engine powering artificial intelligence. While many AI applications might appear to be all about flashy algorithms and futuristic interfaces, the reality is that math provides the essential language and framework for these systems to learn, adapt, and make decisions. In this chapter, we'll take a beginner-friendly journey through the key mathematical concepts that underpin AI. From statistics and probability to linear algebra and calculus, you'll discover how these building blocks come together to create intelligent systems.

Why Math Matters in AI

Imagine trying to build a house without a solid foundation—it wouldn't stand for long. In the same way, without mathematics, AI would be all structure and no substance. Math helps us:

- **Describe Data:** By summarizing and analyzing data, math allows us to capture patterns and trends.

- **Optimize Algorithms:** Calculus and optimization techniques enable AI systems to learn by minimizing errors.

- **Model Complex Systems:** Linear algebra and probability help in representing multi-dimensional data and uncertainty, which are central to AI models.

Even if you're not a math wizard, understanding these concepts—even at a basic level—can greatly enhance your grasp of how AI works.

Statistics: The Language of Data

Descriptive Statistics

Statistics is the branch of math that deals with data—collecting, summarizing, and interpreting it. In AI, descriptive statistics provide a quick snapshot of the data's key characteristics:

- **Mean (Average):** Adds up all data points and divides by the number of points. It gives a central value.

- **Median:** The middle value when data is ordered. Useful for understanding the distribution when outliers are present.

- **Standard Deviation:** Measures how spread out the data is. A small standard deviation indicates that the data points tend to be close to the mean.

For example, when training an AI model on housing prices, knowing the mean and standard deviation can help the model understand what "normal" prices look like and detect unusual trends.

Inferential Statistics

While descriptive statistics tell us what the data looks like, inferential statistics help us make predictions and decisions based on data. Concepts such as:

- **Confidence Intervals:** Provide a range within which we expect the true value to fall.

- **Hypothesis Testing:** Helps determine if a pattern observed in the data is statistically significant or just due to random chance.

These methods are crucial when evaluating the performance of AI models and ensuring that their predictions are reliable.

Probability: Making Sense of Uncertainty

Probability theory is all about quantifying uncertainty—a core aspect of many AI tasks. In a world full of unpredictable events, AI systems use probability to make informed guesses.

Basic Concepts

- **Probability Values:** Range from 0 (impossible event) to 1 (certain event). For instance, flipping a fair coin gives heads a probability of 0.5.

- **Random Variables:** Variables that can take on different values depending on the outcome of a random event. They are used to model uncertainty in AI.

- **Distributions:** Functions that describe the likelihood of different outcomes. The normal (Gaussian) distribution, for example, is widely used because many natural phenomena cluster around an average value.

Bayesian Thinking

One of the most influential frameworks in AI is Bayesian probability. It allows us to update our beliefs based on new data:

- **Prior Probability:** What you initially believe about an event.

- **Likelihood:** How probable the observed data is, given a particular hypothesis.

- **Posterior Probability:** The updated probability after considering the new data.

Bayesian methods are used in various AI applications, such as spam filtering and recommendation systems, where the model must continuously update its predictions based on incoming information.

Linear Algebra: The Building Blocks of Machine Learning

Linear algebra is the study of vectors, matrices, and linear transformations, and it's one of the most fundamental tools in AI.

Vectors and Matrices

- **Vectors:** Think of vectors as lists of numbers that represent data points in space. For example, an image can be represented as a long vector of pixel values.

- **Matrices:** Collections of vectors arranged in rows and columns. They're used to represent datasets, transform data, and perform operations efficiently.

Matrix Operations

- **Addition and Multiplication:** Just like numbers, matrices can be added and multiplied. These operations are crucial for combining data and propagating information through neural networks.

- **Determinants and Inverses:** These concepts help in understanding properties of transformations and are important in algorithms like linear regression.

Applications in AI

In machine learning, linear algebra is used in:

- **Neural Networks:** Weights and biases are

represented as matrices and vectors, and operations such as matrix multiplication drive the forward and backward propagation processes.

- **Dimensionality Reduction:** Techniques like Principal Component Analysis (PCA) reduce the complexity of data by finding the most significant directions (vectors) in high-dimensional space.

Calculus: Understanding Change and Optimization

Calculus, particularly differential calculus, is essential for optimizing AI models. It helps us understand how small changes in input affect the output of a function.

Derivatives

- **What They Represent:** A derivative measures the rate at which a function changes. In AI, derivatives are used to determine how much to adjust a model's parameters (such as weights in a neural network) to minimize errors.

- **Gradient Descent:** A key optimization algorithm that uses the derivative (or gradient) of a function to find its minimum value. By iteratively moving in the direction of the steepest descent, AI models learn to improve their predictions.

Integration

While derivatives measure change, integration helps in calculating areas under curves, which can be useful in probability and in determining cumulative values in datasets.

Optimization in AI

Optimization is at the heart of training AI models. The goal is to minimize a loss function (a measure of error) by adjusting the model's parameters. Calculus provides the mathematical framework to make these adjustments efficiently.

Bringing It All Together in AI

The interplay of statistics, probability, linear algebra, and calculus is what makes modern AI possible:

- **Data Representation:** Statistics and linear algebra work together to represent complex datasets in a structured, analyzable form.

- **Learning from Data:** Probability and statistics help in understanding patterns and making predictions, while calculus and optimization methods adjust model parameters to improve performance.

- **Modeling Complex Systems:** Linear algebra and calculus enable the creation of multi-layered models (such as deep neural networks) that can approximate complex functions and make decisions.

For example, consider training a neural network for image recognition:

1. **Data is represented** as matrices of pixel values.

2. **Statistics help** summarize and preprocess the data.

3. **Linear algebra operations** (like matrix multiplications) move data through the network layers.

4. **Calculus-based optimization** (like gradient descent) fine-tunes the network by minimizing the error between predictions and actual outcomes.

Tools and Resources for Further Learning

While the math behind AI can seem daunting at first, there are many resources available to help you build your skills:

- **Online Courses:** Platforms like Coursera, edX, and Khan Academy offer courses in statistics, linear algebra, and calculus tailored for AI applications.

- **Interactive Tutorials:** Websites such as 3Blue1Brown provide visual and intuitive explanations of key concepts like neural networks and gradient descent.

- **Books:** Consider titles like *"The Elements of Statistical Learning"* or *"Linear Algebra and Its Applications"* to dive deeper into the subject.

- **Practice:** Tools like Jupyter Notebooks and Python libraries (NumPy, Pandas, Matplotlib) allow you to experiment with mathematical concepts through coding.

Conclusion

Mathematics is the unsung hero of artificial intelligence. This chapter has offered a beginner's crash course in the fundamental mathematical concepts that form the backbone of AI. From the descriptive power of statistics and probability's role in managing uncertainty, to the transformative capabilities of linear algebra and calculus in model building and optimization—each area plays a critical role in enabling machines to learn and adapt.

As you continue your journey into AI, remember that these mathematical tools are not just abstract concepts; they are the very language that allows machines to perceive, learn, and make intelligent decisions. Embrace the math, and you'll gain a deeper understanding of the principles that are shaping the technology of tomorrow.

Welcome to the fascinating world where numbers, data, and algorithms converge to unlock the intelligence of tomorrow!

Chapter 11: Exploring Other AI Algorithms

While deep learning, reinforcement learning, and natural language processing have captured much of the spotlight in recent years, the field of artificial intelligence is rich with a diverse array of algorithms that have long powered robust applications across various industries. In this chapter, we'll venture beyond the neural networks and delve into other essential AI algorithms—such as decision trees, clustering methods, support vector machines, and ensemble techniques. These methods offer unique strengths and, in many cases, provide more interpretable or computationally efficient solutions than their deep learning counterparts.

Decision Trees: Branching Out in AI

Imagine you're trying to decide what to wear on a chilly day. You might ask yourself, "Is it cold outside?" If yes, you'd choose a jacket; if no, perhaps a t-shirt will do. This kind of step-by-step reasoning is at the heart of decision trees.

How Decision Trees Work

- **Structure:**
  A decision tree is a flowchart-like structure where each internal node represents a test on an attribute, each branch represents the outcome of that test, and each leaf node represents a final decision or

classification.

- **Interpretability:**
One of the key advantages of decision trees is that they are intuitive and easy to understand. The tree structure mimics human decision-making, making it easier for practitioners to explain how a particular decision was reached.

- **Training Process:**
During training, the algorithm selects the best attribute to split the data at each node. Common criteria for this selection include information gain, Gini impurity, or entropy. The tree grows by recursively partitioning the data until it meets a stopping criterion, such as a maximum depth or a minimum number of samples in a node.

Applications and Use Cases

- **Classification:**
Decision trees can classify data into distinct categories—for example, diagnosing medical conditions based on patient symptoms.

- **Regression:**
They can also be adapted for regression tasks, where the goal is to predict a continuous value, such as housing prices.

- **Real-World Analogy:**
Think of a flowchart used in customer service to

determine the next step in troubleshooting an issue; decision trees function similarly by guiding the process from input to conclusion.

Clustering Methods: Grouping Similarities

Not all problems require a predefined label or outcome. Sometimes, the goal is simply to discover natural groupings within data—a task for which clustering methods are ideally suited.

Understanding Clustering

- **Unsupervised Learning:**
  Clustering is a type of unsupervised learning where the algorithm attempts to group data points based on similarity without prior knowledge of the group labels.

- **Popular Techniques:**

  o **K-Means Clustering:**
    This algorithm partitions data into K clusters by assigning each data point to the nearest cluster center, then iteratively refining the centers based on the mean of the assigned points.

  o **Hierarchical Clustering:**
    In hierarchical clustering, data is organized into a tree-like structure (dendrogram) that

represents nested clusters. This method is particularly useful when the number of clusters is unknown in advance.

- ○ **DBSCAN (Density-Based Spatial Clustering of Applications with Noise):** DBSCAN groups data points that are closely packed together, marking points that lie alone in low-density regions as outliers.

Applications and Benefits

- **Market Segmentation:**
  Businesses use clustering to segment customers based on purchasing behavior, allowing for targeted marketing strategies.

- **Anomaly Detection:**
  Clustering can identify outliers in datasets, such as fraudulent transactions or unusual network activity.

- **Data Exploration:**
  When dealing with large, unlabeled datasets, clustering serves as an invaluable tool for uncovering hidden patterns and insights.

Support Vector Machines: Drawing the Line

Support Vector Machines (SVMs) offer a powerful method for both classification and regression by finding the optimal boundary that separates different classes of data.

The SVM Approach

- **Core Concept:**

  SVMs work by mapping input data into a high-dimensional space and identifying the hyperplane that best separates the classes with the maximum margin. The margin is defined as the distance between the hyperplane and the nearest data point from each class.

- **Kernel Trick:**

  Often, data cannot be separated by a straight line. SVMs overcome this limitation using kernel functions (e.g., polynomial, radial basis function) to transform data into a higher-dimensional space where a linear separator is feasible.

- **Robustness:**

  SVMs are particularly effective in high-dimensional spaces and when the number of dimensions exceeds the number of samples. They are also robust against overfitting, especially in cases where the margin is maximized.

Applications

- **Image Recognition:**

  SVMs have been successfully applied in tasks such as handwriting recognition and facial detection.

- **Bioinformatics:**

  They are used for classifying proteins and genes in

various biological datasets.

- **Text Categorization:**
  SVMs can efficiently categorize text documents, making them useful for spam detection and sentiment analysis.

Ensemble Techniques: The Power of Many

Sometimes, combining multiple algorithms can lead to a more powerful and robust predictive model than any single method on its own. Ensemble techniques do exactly that by aggregating the outputs of several models.

How Ensemble Methods Work

- **Bagging (Bootstrap Aggregating):**
  Bagging involves training multiple instances of the same algorithm on different subsets of the data (sampled with replacement) and then averaging the predictions. Random Forests, an ensemble of decision trees, are a popular example of this technique.

- **Boosting:**
  Boosting focuses on training a series of models where each subsequent model attempts to correct the errors of its predecessor. Algorithms like AdaBoost and Gradient Boosting fall into this category.

- **Voting and Stacking:**
  These techniques combine the predictions of diverse models. In voting, each model casts a "vote" for the final prediction, while stacking involves training a meta-model to aggregate the predictions from multiple base models.

Advantages and Real-World Examples

- **Improved Accuracy:**
  By leveraging the strengths of multiple models, ensembles often achieve higher accuracy and generalize better to unseen data.

- **Versatility:**
  Ensemble methods can be applied across various domains, from predicting stock market trends to diagnosing diseases.

- **Intuitive Analogy:**
  Consider how a panel of experts might make a more balanced decision than a single specialist. Ensemble methods work similarly by combining multiple "opinions" (models) to reach a final decision.

Other Notable Algorithms and Techniques

Beyond the methods discussed above, there are additional algorithms that play vital roles in AI:

- **Dimensionality Reduction Techniques:**
  Methods like Principal Component Analysis (PCA) and t-Distributed Stochastic Neighbor Embedding (t-SNE) help simplify high-dimensional data, making it easier to visualize and process.

- **Bayesian Networks:**
  These probabilistic graphical models represent a set of variables and their conditional dependencies via a directed acyclic graph. They are particularly useful for reasoning under uncertainty.

- **Genetic Algorithms:**
  Inspired by the process of natural selection, genetic algorithms are used to solve optimization problems by iteratively selecting, combining, and mutating candidate solutions.

Each of these techniques has its own set of advantages and is suited for different types of challenges, further enriching the toolbox available to AI practitioners.

Choosing the Right Algorithm

In practice, there is no one-size-fits-all solution. The choice of algorithm depends on several factors, including:

- **Nature of the Data:**
  Is your data labeled or unlabeled? High-dimensional or sparse? Structured or unstructured?

- **Interpretability:**
  Do you need a model that can be easily explained to stakeholders, or is predictive performance the sole priority?

- **Computational Resources:**
  Some algorithms are more computationally intensive than others. Consider the available resources and time constraints.

- **Specific Application Needs:**
  Different tasks—be it classification, regression, or clustering—may favor different algorithms.

Experimentation and validation are key. Often, practitioners try multiple algorithms, evaluate their performance, and select the one that best meets the requirements of the task at hand.

Conclusion

Exploring the diverse range of AI algorithms reveals a vibrant ecosystem of methods that extend well beyond the realm of deep learning and neural networks. Decision trees offer transparency and ease of interpretation; clustering methods excel in uncovering hidden structures in data; support vector machines provide robust performance in high-dimensional spaces; and ensemble techniques harness the collective wisdom of multiple models to boost accuracy.

Understanding these algorithms not only broadens your perspective on AI but also equips you with the tools to tackle a variety of problems in innovative ways. Each algorithm has its unique strengths and is suited for specific scenarios, emphasizing that the art of AI is as much about choosing the right approach as it is about designing sophisticated models.

As you continue your journey into the intelligence of tomorrow, remember that the power of AI lies in its diversity. Embrace the wide array of algorithms at your disposal, and you'll be well-prepared to unlock solutions to the most complex and exciting challenges in the world of artificial intelligence.

Chapter 12: Big Data: Fuel for the AI Engine

In today's digital age, data is everywhere—streaming in from social media, sensors, transactions, and countless other sources. This massive influx of information, known as Big Data, serves as the critical fuel that powers modern AI. In this chapter, we will explore what Big Data is, how it is collected, stored, and processed, and why it is indispensable for training AI systems. We'll also discuss the challenges and future prospects of working with such vast quantities of information.

What Is Big Data?

Big Data refers to data sets that are so large, complex, and fast-moving that traditional data processing methods struggle to handle them effectively. The concept is often encapsulated by the "Three Vs":

- **Volume:**
  The sheer amount of data generated every second—from social media posts to sensor readings—requires storage solutions and processing techniques that can handle terabytes, petabytes, or even exabytes of information.

- **Velocity:**
  Data is not only vast in quantity but also generated at high speed. Real-time data streams from online transactions, stock markets, and connected devices

demand immediate processing and analysis.

- **Variety:**
  Big Data encompasses a wide range of formats. It includes structured data (like spreadsheets and relational databases), semi-structured data (like JSON and XML files), and unstructured data (such as text, images, and videos).

Additional characteristics, such as **Veracity** (the quality and reliability of data) and **Value** (the insights and benefits derived from data), further illustrate the multifaceted nature of Big Data.

Sources and Collection of Big Data

Big Data is sourced from nearly every aspect of modern life. Here are some of the most common sources:

- **Social Media Platforms:**
  Sites like Facebook, Twitter, and Instagram generate massive amounts of text, image, and video data, reflecting human behavior, trends, and interactions.

- **Sensors and IoT Devices:**
  From smart home devices to industrial sensors, the Internet of Things (IoT) produces continuous streams of data that provide real-time insights into operations and environmental conditions.

- **Transactional Systems:**
  Financial transactions, e-commerce purchases, and other business operations create structured datasets that are critical for understanding consumer behavior and market dynamics.

- **Multimedia Content:**
  Videos, images, and audio recordings are increasingly important in areas such as surveillance, entertainment, and digital marketing, requiring sophisticated techniques for analysis.

- **Scientific Research:**
  Fields such as genomics, astronomy, and climate science generate data at scales that push the limits of conventional processing, driving the need for specialized Big Data solutions.

The effective collection of this data requires a combination of sensors, APIs, and web scraping tools, as well as robust strategies to ensure that data is captured reliably and ethically.

Data Storage and Processing

Storing and processing Big Data necessitate innovative technologies designed to handle its volume and variety:

Distributed Storage Systems

- **Hadoop Distributed File System (HDFS):**
  HDFS is designed to store very large files across multiple machines, providing redundancy and high availability. It forms the backbone of many Big Data solutions.

- **NoSQL Databases:**
  Databases like MongoDB, Cassandra, and HBase are tailored to handle unstructured or semi-structured data, offering scalability and flexibility beyond traditional relational databases.

Data Processing Frameworks

- **Apache Hadoop:**
  Hadoop is an ecosystem that includes tools for distributed storage (HDFS) and processing (MapReduce). It enables the parallel processing of vast datasets.

- **Apache Spark:**
  Spark is a fast and general-purpose cluster-computing framework that allows for in-memory processing of Big Data, significantly speeding up tasks such as iterative machine learning and real-time analytics.

Data Cleaning and Preprocessing

Before Big Data can be used to train AI models, it must be cleaned and preprocessed to ensure quality and consistency. This involves:

- **Data Cleansing:**
  Removing duplicates, handling missing values, and correcting errors to improve data quality.

- **Normalization and Transformation:**
  Standardizing data formats and scales to ensure compatibility across different systems and algorithms.

- **Feature Extraction:**
  Identifying and extracting the relevant features from raw data that will be used to train machine learning models.

Effective preprocessing is critical; even the most advanced AI models can yield poor results if the underlying data is noisy or biased.

Big Data's Role in AI

Big Data and AI are intertwined—each drives the advancement of the other in a synergistic relationship:

Training Powerful Models

AI models, especially those based on deep learning, require enormous amounts of data to learn complex patterns. For example:

- **Image Recognition:**
  Deep neural networks trained on millions of labeled

images can recognize objects with high accuracy.

- **Natural Language Processing:**
  Large text corpora enable AI systems to understand language context, sentiment, and nuances, powering applications like translation and conversational agents.

Enhancing Decision-Making

By leveraging Big Data, AI systems can provide insights that inform decision-making in real-time. In fields such as finance and healthcare, AI algorithms analyze massive datasets to detect trends, forecast outcomes, and identify anomalies.

Personalized Experiences

From targeted advertising to personalized recommendations on streaming services, AI uses Big Data to tailor experiences to individual preferences, improving user satisfaction and engagement.

Challenges in Managing Big Data

While Big Data offers tremendous opportunities, it also poses significant challenges:

Data Quality and Veracity

Not all data is created equal. Inaccurate, incomplete, or biased data can lead to misleading insights and flawed AI models. Ensuring data veracity is essential for building reliable systems.

Scalability and Performance

Processing and storing massive datasets require robust infrastructure. As data volumes grow, systems must scale efficiently to maintain performance without incurring prohibitive costs.

Privacy and Security

Collecting and analyzing large amounts of personal data raises serious privacy and security concerns. Regulations such as GDPR impose strict guidelines on data handling, necessitating transparent and secure data practices.

Integration and Interoperability

Big Data often originates from diverse sources and in different formats. Integrating these disparate datasets into a cohesive whole requires sophisticated tools and standardized protocols.

The Future of Big Data in AI

The relationship between Big Data and AI is set to deepen as both fields evolve. Here are some emerging trends:

- **Real-Time Analytics:**
  Advances in processing power and distributed computing are paving the way for real-time Big Data

analytics, enabling AI systems to react instantaneously to new information.

- **Edge Computing:**
  As more devices become connected, processing data at the edge (close to the source) will reduce latency and improve efficiency, especially in applications like autonomous vehicles and smart cities.

- **Enhanced Data Governance:**
  Future developments will likely focus on improving data quality, privacy, and security, ensuring that Big Data remains a trustworthy resource for AI.

- **Integration of Diverse Data Types:**
  Improved methodologies for fusing data from various sources—text, images, video, sensor data—will create richer, more informative datasets that drive even more sophisticated AI models.

Conclusion

Big Data is much more than just an overwhelming volume of information—it is the lifeblood that fuels the development and refinement of AI systems. By enabling the collection, storage, and analysis of vast amounts of data, Big Data has opened new frontiers in machine learning, personalized services, and real-time decision-making. However, harnessing this potential requires addressing challenges related to data quality, scalability, and privacy.

As you continue your journey into the world of AI, remember that Big Data is not just about quantity—it's about extracting meaningful insights that empower intelligent systems to learn, adapt, and transform our world. Embrace the challenges and opportunities that Big Data presents, and you'll gain a deeper appreciation for its role as the fuel driving the intelligence of tomorrow.

Welcome to the era of Big Data—a realm where every byte holds the promise of unlocking new levels of intelligence and innovation!

Chapter 13: AI in Everyday Life

Artificial Intelligence is no longer confined to futuristic labs or science fiction novels—it has seamlessly woven itself into the fabric of our daily lives. In this chapter, we explore how AI impacts everyday activities, transforming routine tasks into smarter, more efficient processes. From the moment you wake up until you go to bed, AI influences how you interact with technology, make decisions, and even entertain yourself. Let's take a closer look at the omnipresence of AI in our world.

The Ubiquity of AI: An Invisible Helper

Consider your daily routine. Even if you aren't aware of it, AI is likely assisting you at every turn:

- **Morning Routine:**
  Your smartphone's alarm app might adjust wake-up times based on your sleep patterns, while a smart mirror could offer personalized news and weather updates.

- **Commute and Navigation:**
  AI-driven navigation apps analyze traffic in real time, suggesting the fastest routes and adjusting for unexpected road conditions. In some cities, public transportation systems use AI to optimize schedules and manage capacity.

- **Work and Productivity:**
  Email clients filter spam, calendars schedule meetings automatically, and virtual assistants help organize your day. AI-powered tools even provide insights from large datasets to support business decisions.

These examples illustrate that AI is no longer an abstract concept—it is an integral, yet often invisible, part of modern living.

AI in Communication and Social Interaction

Smart Communication Tools

- **Virtual Assistants:**
  Voice-activated assistants like Siri, Alexa, and Google Assistant help you send messages, set reminders, and answer questions—all through simple voice commands.

- **Chatbots and Customer Service:**
  When you chat with a customer service bot online, you're interacting with an AI system that understands your query and provides real-time assistance. These bots learn from countless interactions to improve their responses over time.

- **Language Translation:**
  AI-powered translation apps break down language

barriers by providing instant, context-aware translations for both written text and speech, making global communication more accessible than ever.

Social Media and Content Curation

- **Personalized Feeds:**
  Social media platforms leverage AI to curate content based on your interests, ensuring that the posts, articles, and videos you see are relevant and engaging.

- **Content Moderation:**
  AI algorithms help detect and filter harmful content, protecting users from spam, hate speech, or misinformation while maintaining vibrant online communities.

These communication tools not only make our interactions more efficient but also enable us to connect with a broader world in meaningful ways.

AI in the Home: Smart Living Made Simple

Smart Home Devices

- **Home Automation:**
  Smart thermostats adjust temperatures based on your habits, and AI-enabled lighting systems create moods by automatically dimming or brightening

lights. These devices learn your preferences over time, offering both comfort and energy savings.

- **Security and Surveillance:**
  AI-powered cameras and doorbells recognize familiar faces, detect unusual activities, and send alerts directly to your phone, ensuring a higher level of home security.

- **Voice-Activated Control:**
  Whether you're controlling the music in your living room or managing your smart appliances, AI makes it possible to operate your home with simple voice commands or intuitive gestures.

Entertainment and Media

- **Streaming Services:**
  AI algorithms analyze your viewing and listening habits to recommend movies, TV shows, and music that match your taste, turning entertainment into a highly personalized experience.

- **Gaming:**
  Modern video games use AI to create adaptive challenges and lifelike non-player characters (NPCs) that respond intelligently to your actions, making gameplay more immersive and engaging.

The integration of AI in the home not only enhances convenience and comfort but also creates an environment that adapts to your lifestyle.

AI on the Go: Transportation and Navigation

Smarter Commuting

- **Navigation Systems:**
  Real-time data processing helps navigation apps suggest alternate routes, avoid traffic jams, and even predict travel times based on historical data and current conditions.

- **Ride-Sharing Services:**
  Platforms like Uber and Lyft use AI to match drivers with riders, optimize routes, and adjust prices based on demand, ensuring efficient and dynamic transportation options.

- **Autonomous Vehicles:**
  While still in development and early adoption phases, self-driving cars use a combination of computer vision, sensor fusion, and machine learning to navigate roads safely. These vehicles promise to reduce accidents, improve traffic flow, and provide mobility for those unable to drive.

Public Transportation

- **Optimized Schedules:**
  Many cities are integrating AI to analyze commuter patterns, enabling public transit systems to adjust schedules and routes in real time. This responsiveness helps reduce wait times and overcrowding.

- **Safety Enhancements:**
  AI-driven monitoring systems in trains and buses help identify and respond to safety issues, such as detecting unusual behavior or equipment malfunctions before they escalate.

Transportation, empowered by AI, is becoming more reliable, safer, and tailored to the needs of urban dwellers.

AI in Health and Wellbeing

Personal Health Management

- **Wearable Devices:**
  Fitness trackers and smartwatches use AI to monitor your heart rate, track your physical activity, and even detect irregularities in your sleep patterns. These devices empower you to manage your health proactively.

- **Virtual Health Assistants:**
  AI-powered apps offer personalized advice on diet, exercise, and mental wellness based on your individual data, helping you maintain a balanced lifestyle.

Healthcare Services

- **Diagnostics and Imaging:**
  AI algorithms assist doctors in analyzing medical images such as X-rays and MRIs, often detecting

conditions at an early stage and with high accuracy.

- **Telemedicine:**
  With AI enhancing the capabilities of remote consultations, patients can receive preliminary diagnoses and care recommendations from the comfort of their homes.

By integrating AI into health and wellbeing, the gap between patients and quality healthcare is steadily narrowing, leading to earlier diagnoses and more personalized treatment plans.

AI in Finance and Daily Transactions

Smarter Financial Services

- **Fraud Detection:**
  Banks and credit card companies use AI to analyze transaction patterns and flag unusual activities that may indicate fraud, protecting your financial assets.

- **Personalized Banking:**
  AI-driven financial apps provide tailored advice, helping you manage budgets, track spending, and even plan investments based on your unique financial situation.

- **Automated Services:**
  Routine transactions, from bill payments to money transfers, are streamlined through AI, reducing

processing times and enhancing security.

E-Commerce and Shopping

- **Recommendation Systems:**
  Online retailers leverage AI to suggest products based on your browsing and purchase history, creating a shopping experience that feels both personal and intuitive.

- **Inventory Management:**
  Behind the scenes, AI optimizes stock levels and supply chain logistics, ensuring that products are available when you need them and reducing waste.

In finance and commerce, AI not only enhances the convenience of transactions but also improves security and personalization, making everyday financial management easier and more efficient.

Conclusion: Embracing an AI-Enhanced Lifestyle

Artificial Intelligence is not a distant future—it's here, transforming the minutiae of our daily lives. From the moment you wake up to the time you rest, AI works quietly in the background to improve your safety, convenience, and overall quality of life. It's the invisible force behind smart homes, efficient transportation, personalized healthcare, and intelligent financial services.

As you continue to navigate this AI-enhanced world,

consider how these innovations not only simplify routine tasks but also open up new possibilities for creativity, connection, and improved wellbeing. The everyday applications of AI are a testament to its transformative power, making life more efficient, enjoyable, and accessible for everyone.

Welcome to the everyday revolution of artificial intelligence—a world where every interaction, every device, and every decision is a step toward a smarter, more connected future!

Chapter 14: The Creative Side of AI

In the realm of artificial intelligence, creativity might seem like a human-exclusive domain—a mysterious spark of ingenuity that sets us apart from machines. Yet, in recent years, AI has made impressive inroads into creative endeavors, from painting and music composition to writing and beyond. In this chapter, we explore how AI is challenging traditional notions of creativity, enabling new forms of artistic expression, and even collaborating with human creators to produce innovative works. Prepare to embark on a journey that blurs the line between human imagination and machine-generated art.

The Intersection of Creativity and Technology

Creativity has long been celebrated as a distinctly human trait, associated with emotion, intuition, and personal experience. However, as computers have become more powerful and algorithms more sophisticated, they have also started to exhibit behaviors that can be described as creative. AI-driven systems can now analyze vast amounts of data, learn from historical artistic trends, and generate novel outputs that sometimes rival or even inspire human works.

- **Redefining Creativity:**
  Rather than replacing human creativity, AI serves as a tool that extends our creative capabilities. It offers

new methods for exploring ideas and reimagining artistic forms.

- **Collaboration Between Man and Machine:** Increasingly, artists and musicians are partnering with AI to push the boundaries of what is possible. These collaborations yield unexpected results— hybrid works where human vision is enhanced by the algorithm's ability to analyze and generate patterns.

AI in Visual Arts

AI-Generated Art

One of the most visually striking applications of AI is in the field of visual arts. Algorithms such as Generative Adversarial Networks (GANs) have been used to create paintings, digital art, and even sculptures that are both original and evocative.

- **Generative Adversarial Networks (GANs):** GANs consist of two neural networks—a generator and a discriminator—that work in tandem to produce images that resemble real artworks. The generator creates new images while the discriminator evaluates them against a dataset of existing art. Over time, the generator learns to produce increasingly convincing images. Some pieces produced by GANs have even been sold at prestigious auctions, sparking debates about the nature of art and creativity.

- **Style Transfer:**
  Another popular technique is style transfer, where AI takes the content of one image and applies the artistic style of another. Imagine a photograph transformed to mimic the brushstrokes of Van Gogh or the abstract forms of Picasso. This process allows artists to experiment with visual styles that they might not otherwise have the skill or time to master.

Beyond Traditional Canvas

AI is not confined to creating static images. It has also ventured into interactive installations and dynamic visual experiences:

- **Interactive Exhibitions:**
  Museums and galleries around the world are hosting exhibitions where AI-generated art responds to viewer input in real time, creating an immersive experience that blurs the boundaries between artist and audience.

- **Digital Sculptures and 3D Art:**
  With advances in 3D modeling and virtual reality, AI is now used to design digital sculptures and immersive environments that challenge our perceptions of space and form.

AI in Music Composition

Music is another arena where AI has shown remarkable creative potential. From composing symphonies to generating beats for contemporary tracks, AI is proving to be an invaluable collaborator in the musical landscape.

Composing Music with AI

- **Algorithmic Composition:**
  Early experiments in AI music involved rule-based systems that could compose simple melodies. Today's AI composers use deep learning to analyze thousands of pieces of music, learning patterns and structures that they then employ to generate entirely new compositions. These algorithms can compose in a variety of styles, from classical to electronic, often producing pieces that are indistinguishable from those written by human composers.

- **Adaptive Soundtracks:**
  In the world of video games and interactive media, AI is being used to create adaptive soundtracks that change in response to the player's actions. This dynamic music enhances immersion by ensuring that the soundtrack evolves in tandem with the unfolding narrative or gameplay.

Collaborative Creation

- **Human-AI Duets:**
  Musicians are experimenting with AI as a partner in live performances. Some artists use AI-generated suggestions as a springboard for improvisation, leading to duets where the human and the machine trade musical ideas in real time.

- **Remixing and Sampling:**
  AI tools can also analyze and remix existing music. By identifying patterns, beats, and motifs within a track, these systems can suggest new combinations or even create entirely new versions of a song, offering fresh perspectives on familiar melodies.

AI in Literature and Writing

The written word is another frontier where AI is making a bold impact. Advanced language models are now capable of generating text that ranges from poetry and short stories to news articles and technical reports.

Generative Writing Models

- **Language Models:**
  Models such as GPT (Generative Pre-trained Transformer) have been trained on vast corpora of text, enabling them to generate coherent, contextually relevant passages of writing. These

systems can produce creative content that mimics the style of specific authors or genres, opening up exciting possibilities for experimental literature.

- **Collaborative Storytelling:**
  AI is increasingly used as a co-writer. Authors may input prompts or partial drafts into an AI system, which then offers suggestions, completes sentences, or even develops entire plotlines. This form of collaboration can help overcome writer's block, generate new ideas, and experiment with narrative structures that might be too unconventional to conceive independently.

The Impact on Publishing and Journalism

- **Content Creation:**
  AI is already being used in newsrooms to draft reports on sports, finance, and weather. While these applications focus on efficiency and factual reporting, creative writing models are pushing the envelope of what's possible in narrative journalism and fiction.

- **Ethical and Creative Debates:**
  The rise of AI-generated literature has sparked debates about authorship, originality, and intellectual property. Who owns a story written by a machine? Can an AI truly be creative, or is it simply remixing patterns from existing texts? These

questions continue to fuel discussions among writers, publishers, and technologists.

Other Creative Domains: Beyond Art, Music, and Literature

Film and Animation

AI is also making waves in the film industry. From scriptwriting and storyboarding to visual effects and animation, AI tools are being integrated into various stages of film production.

- **Script Analysis:**
  AI can analyze film scripts to predict audience reactions, assess narrative structures, and even suggest improvements.

- **Visual Effects:**
  In post-production, AI algorithms are used to enhance visual effects, color grading, and even to create realistic digital characters that blend seamlessly with live-action footage.

Fashion and Design

- **Fashion Innovation:**
  Designers are using AI to predict trends, generate new clothing designs, and create custom-fit garments. Algorithms can analyze social media and sales data to forecast what styles will be popular in

upcoming seasons.

- **Interior and Product Design:**
AI tools help architects and designers create innovative spaces and products by simulating various design elements and optimizing for aesthetics and functionality.

Debating Creativity: Machines vs. Humans

The creative prowess of AI invites philosophical and ethical questions about the nature of creativity itself.

- **Authenticity and Emotion:**
Critics argue that while AI can mimic creative processes, it lacks the emotional depth and subjective experience that characterize human creativity. Can a machine, which does not experience life, truly create art that resonates on a human level?

- **Augmentation, Not Replacement:**
Many experts see AI as a complement to human creativity rather than a replacement. By handling repetitive tasks or suggesting novel ideas, AI can free human creators to focus on the deeper, more intuitive aspects of their work.

- **Redefining Art:**
The integration of AI into creative fields challenges

traditional definitions of art and authorship. As AI-generated works gain recognition, society must consider how to value and attribute creative output in a digital age.

The Future of Creativity in an AI World

Looking ahead, the creative landscape is poised to evolve dramatically as AI technologies continue to mature.

- **Enhanced Collaboration:**
  Future systems may offer even more seamless collaboration between human creators and AI, with tools that understand individual creative styles and preferences.

- **New Art Forms:**
  As AI expands its creative capabilities, entirely new art forms may emerge—blending digital, interactive, and augmented reality experiences that challenge our conventional notions of art.

- **Accessibility and Democratization:**
  AI has the potential to democratize creativity, providing tools and platforms that allow people without formal training to express themselves artistically. This could lead to a more diverse and vibrant cultural landscape.

- **Ethical and Societal Considerations:**
  As with all technology, the integration of AI into creative fields will require ongoing dialogue about ethics, intellectual property, and the social impact of automated creativity. Balancing innovation with respect for human expression will be a central challenge in the years to come.

Conclusion

The creative side of AI opens up a world where machines and humans work in tandem to push the boundaries of artistic expression. Whether generating stunning visual art, composing emotive music, or crafting engaging stories, AI is proving that creativity is not solely the domain of human experience. Instead, it is emerging as a shared space—one where algorithms become collaborators and new forms of art are born from the interplay of data and imagination.

As you continue to explore the intelligence of tomorrow, consider how AI is not only solving practical problems but also inspiring beauty, innovation, and a redefinition of what it means to be creative. The future of art, music, literature, and beyond is a dynamic canvas painted with the combined brushes of human ingenuity and machine learning.

Welcome to the creative revolution of artificial

intelligence—a world where every algorithm holds the potential to inspire, every code can spark innovation, and every collaboration between man and machine expands the horizons of artistic possibility!

Chapter 15: Ethics in AI: Navigating the Moral Landscape

As artificial intelligence becomes an integral part of our lives, its impact extends beyond technical innovation to touch on deeply human questions of ethics and morality. In this chapter, we delve into the ethical challenges and responsibilities that come with designing and deploying AI systems. We will explore issues such as bias, privacy, accountability, and the broader societal implications of AI. By examining both the risks and the opportunities, this chapter aims to provide a balanced perspective on how to navigate the moral landscape of artificial intelligence.

The Importance of Ethics in AI

Artificial intelligence holds the promise of transforming industries, solving complex problems, and improving everyday life. However, with great power comes great responsibility. As AI systems become more autonomous and influential, they also raise critical ethical questions:

- **Fairness and Bias:**
  AI systems learn from data that reflect historical and societal biases. Without careful design and oversight, these systems can perpetuate or even amplify unfair treatment of certain groups.

- **Privacy and Surveillance:**
  The data that fuel AI can include sensitive personal

information. Balancing the benefits of data-driven insights with the protection of individual privacy is an ongoing challenge.

- **Transparency and Accountability:**
  AI models, especially those based on deep learning, often operate as "black boxes" with decisions that are difficult to explain. This lack of transparency can complicate accountability, particularly in high-stakes areas like healthcare, criminal justice, and finance.

- **Autonomy and Control:**
  As AI systems gain decision-making power, questions arise about the extent to which humans should delegate control. Determining where to draw the line between human oversight and machine autonomy is critical for ethical governance.

Understanding these issues is not only a technical necessity—it is a moral imperative. Ethical AI can help ensure that technology serves the public good and respects human dignity.

Key Ethical Challenges in AI

Bias and Fairness

One of the most pressing concerns in AI ethics is bias. Since AI systems learn from historical data, they may inherit and even exacerbate existing inequalities.

- **Sources of Bias:**
  Bias can originate from skewed data collection, historical prejudices, or even the design of the algorithm itself. For example, facial recognition systems have been found to have higher error rates for people with darker skin tones, reflecting biases in training data.

- **Mitigation Strategies:**
  To address bias, researchers are developing techniques for fairness-aware machine learning. These include:

  - **Data Auditing:** Evaluating datasets for representativeness and fairness before training models.

  - **Algorithmic Adjustments:** Modifying algorithms to correct for imbalances and ensure equitable treatment.

  - **Inclusive Design:** Involving diverse groups in the design and testing process to uncover and address potential biases.

By proactively addressing bias, AI developers can work toward systems that make fair decisions and foster trust among users.

Privacy and Data Protection

The power of AI often hinges on access to large volumes of data, much of which can be personal or sensitive. This raises significant privacy concerns.

- **Data Collection and Consent:**
  Ethical AI requires transparency about what data is collected, how it is used, and who has access to it. Users must have a clear understanding and control over their personal information.

- **Anonymization and Security:**
  Techniques such as data anonymization and encryption help protect privacy by ensuring that individual identities are not easily inferred from datasets. However, these methods must be robust enough to guard against re-identification attacks.

- **Regulatory Frameworks:**
  Laws such as the European Union's General Data Protection Regulation (GDPR) set standards for data privacy and require companies to implement measures that protect personal information. Adhering to these regulations is essential for ethical AI deployment.

Balancing innovation with privacy protection is essential to maintain public trust and safeguard individual rights.

Transparency and Explainability

For AI systems to be trusted and accountable, their decision-making processes must be understandable to humans.

- **The Black Box Problem:**
  Many advanced AI models, particularly deep neural networks, are inherently complex and operate in ways that are not easily interpretable. This opacity can hinder efforts to understand why a particular decision was made.

- **Explainable AI (XAI):**
  Researchers are actively developing methods to create more interpretable models. Techniques such as feature importance mapping, model simplification, and surrogate models aim to shed light on the inner workings of AI.

- **Accountability Mechanisms:**
  Ensuring that AI decisions can be audited and explained is critical, especially in sectors where decisions have significant consequences. Clear documentation, rigorous testing, and transparent reporting practices contribute to greater accountability.

By making AI systems more transparent, developers can build models that not only perform well but also justify their decisions in ways that humans can understand.

Responsibility and Governance

As AI systems increasingly influence critical aspects of society, establishing clear lines of responsibility becomes paramount.

- **Human Oversight:**
  It is essential to maintain human oversight over AI decisions, especially in high-risk domains such as criminal justice or healthcare. Humans must remain accountable for decisions made with the assistance of AI.

- **Ethical Frameworks and Standards:**
  Organizations and governments are working to develop ethical guidelines and industry standards for AI. These frameworks aim to ensure that AI is developed and deployed in ways that prioritize public welfare and minimize harm.

- **Global Cooperation:**
  The challenges of AI ethics are not confined to any one country or culture. International collaboration and dialogue are crucial to developing ethical standards that are globally recognized and enforced.

Establishing robust governance structures helps ensure that the benefits of AI are realized without compromising ethical standards or societal values.

Real-World Implications and Case Studies

Healthcare

In healthcare, AI holds great promise for improving diagnostics and personalizing treatment. However, ethical concerns about data privacy, consent, and the potential for biased outcomes are particularly acute.

- **Case Study:**
  An AI system designed to assist in diagnosing diseases must be trained on diverse datasets to ensure it works effectively across different populations. Failure to do so can result in misdiagnosis or unequal treatment outcomes.

Criminal Justice

AI tools are increasingly used in criminal justice for tasks such as risk assessment and predictive policing. The ethical stakes are high, as biased or opaque algorithms can lead to unjust outcomes.

- **Case Study:**
  Predictive policing systems have been criticized for disproportionately targeting minority communities. Ethical AI development in this area requires rigorous evaluation of the training data, ongoing monitoring for bias, and clear channels for accountability and redress.

Finance

In finance, AI-driven algorithms can improve efficiency and detect fraudulent activities. However, lack of transparency in decision-making can lead to unfair lending practices or unintentional discrimination.

- **Case Study:**
  Credit scoring systems must be carefully designed to avoid inadvertently penalizing certain demographics. Transparent algorithms and regular audits help ensure that lending decisions are fair and unbiased.

The Path Forward: Towards Ethical AI

Moving forward, integrating ethics into the AI development lifecycle is not optional—it is essential for building systems that benefit society as a whole.

- **Education and Awareness:**
  Developers, stakeholders, and users alike must be educated about the ethical implications of AI. Incorporating ethics into computer science curricula and ongoing professional training can foster a culture of responsibility.

- **Interdisciplinary Collaboration:**
  Solving ethical challenges in AI requires input from diverse fields, including philosophy, law, sociology,

and computer science. Collaboration across disciplines can lead to more holistic and effective ethical frameworks.

- **Continuous Evaluation:**
Ethical considerations must be revisited throughout the lifecycle of an AI system. Ongoing monitoring, regular audits, and adaptive policies help ensure that AI remains aligned with evolving societal values and expectations.

- **Public Engagement:**
Open dialogue with the public is critical. By involving communities in the conversation about AI ethics, developers and policymakers can ensure that the technology reflects the needs and values of the people it is meant to serve.

Conclusion

Ethics in AI is a complex, multifaceted challenge that touches every aspect of technology design, deployment, and governance. As we navigate the moral landscape of AI, it is imperative to address issues of bias, privacy, transparency, and accountability with rigor and sensitivity. By fostering an environment of ethical awareness, interdisciplinary collaboration, and continuous oversight, we can harness the power of AI while safeguarding human rights and societal values.

The journey toward ethical AI is ongoing, demanding vigilance, adaptation, and a steadfast commitment to the public good. As you continue your exploration of artificial intelligence, remember that technology is most powerful when it uplifts humanity—balancing innovation with ethical responsibility will ensure that AI truly serves as a force for positive change.

Welcome to the ethical frontier of artificial intelligence—a domain where every algorithm is scrutinized, every decision is accountable, and every step forward is measured against the values that define our shared humanity.

Chapter 16: Bias and Fairness: Ensuring Equitable AI

Artificial Intelligence has the potential to transform our world for the better, but it also carries the risk of perpetuating existing inequalities. Bias and fairness are critical considerations in AI development because the data and algorithms we build can reflect and even amplify societal prejudices. In this chapter, we explore how bias arises in AI, the various dimensions of fairness, and the strategies that researchers and practitioners can employ to ensure that AI systems are equitable and just.

Understanding Bias in AI

Bias in AI refers to systematic errors that lead to unfair outcomes for certain groups or individuals. These biases can creep into AI systems at multiple stages—from data collection and preparation to algorithm design and deployment.

Sources of Bias

- **Data Bias:**
  AI systems learn from historical data that often reflects societal imbalances. If certain groups are underrepresented or misrepresented in the training data, the AI's predictions and decisions will likely mirror these disparities.

- **Algorithmic Bias:**
  The design of an algorithm itself can introduce bias. When developers make choices about model architecture, features, or optimization criteria, these decisions can inadvertently favor one group over another.

- **User Interaction Bias:**
  AI systems that learn from user behavior may pick up on existing biases. For example, if a recommendation system learns from biased click-through data, it can reinforce stereotypes or filter bubbles.

Real-World Consequences

Bias in AI can have significant and tangible impacts:

- **Employment:** Algorithms used in recruitment may filter out qualified candidates from underrepresented groups.

- **Criminal Justice:** Predictive policing tools may disproportionately target minority communities, leading to over-policing and wrongful arrests.

- **Healthcare:** Biased diagnostic tools can result in misdiagnoses or inadequate treatment for certain populations.

Understanding the sources and impacts of bias is the first step toward mitigating its effects in AI systems.

Defining Fairness in AI

Fairness in AI is a multifaceted concept that involves ensuring that AI systems operate equitably and do not discriminate against individuals or groups. There is no one-size-fits-all definition of fairness; instead, it depends on the context and the values of the society in which the AI is deployed.

Dimensions of Fairness

- **Group Fairness:**
  This concept focuses on ensuring that different demographic groups (e.g., based on race, gender, or age) receive similar outcomes from an AI system. Metrics like demographic parity and equal opportunity fall under this category.

- **Individual Fairness:**
  Individual fairness emphasizes that similar individuals should be treated similarly by an AI system. This approach requires defining a notion of similarity between individuals and ensuring that the model's outputs are consistent for those who are alike.

- **Procedural Fairness:**
  Beyond outcomes, procedural fairness concerns the fairness of the processes and methodologies used to develop and deploy AI. This includes transparency in algorithm design, accountability in decision-

making, and the inclusion of diverse perspectives in the development process.

Fairness Metrics

To measure fairness, researchers have developed several metrics:

- **Statistical Parity:**
  Checks whether different groups have equal probabilities of receiving a positive outcome.

- **Equalized Odds:**
  Ensures that true positive and false positive rates are similar across groups.

- **Calibration:**
  Evaluates whether predictions are equally reliable for different groups.

These metrics provide a framework for quantifying fairness, though choosing the right metric often depends on the specific application and societal context.

Strategies for Mitigating Bias

Mitigating bias in AI requires a holistic approach, addressing both data and algorithmic challenges.

Improving Data Quality

- **Data Auditing:**
  Regularly evaluate datasets for representativeness and fairness. Identify and address gaps where certain groups might be underrepresented.

- **Data Augmentation:**
  Supplement existing datasets with additional data that represents underrepresented groups to create a more balanced training set.

- **Anonymization and De-biasing:**
  Techniques like anonymization help reduce the influence of sensitive attributes, while algorithmic de-biasing can adjust the data to minimize skewed representations.

Algorithmic Interventions

- **Fairness-Aware Learning:**
  Incorporate fairness constraints directly into the learning algorithm. For example, modify the objective function to penalize unfair outcomes.

- **Adversarial Debiasing:**
  Use adversarial techniques where one model learns to make predictions while another tries to predict sensitive attributes. The primary model is penalized if the sensitive attributes can be predicted, encouraging it to ignore biasing features.

- **Post-Processing Corrections:**
  After a model is trained, adjust its outputs to ensure fairness. Techniques such as re-weighting predictions can help balance the outcomes for different groups.

Transparent and Inclusive Development

- **Interdisciplinary Collaboration:**
  Engage experts from diverse fields—such as ethics, law, and social sciences—to provide insights into potential biases and fairness concerns.

- **Stakeholder Involvement:**
  Involve the communities that will be affected by the AI system in its design and evaluation. Public consultations and feedback loops can help align the technology with societal values.

- **Continuous Monitoring:**
  Implement ongoing audits and monitoring systems to detect and address biases as the AI system is used in real-world scenarios.

By combining technical interventions with transparent, inclusive processes, developers can create AI systems that are not only effective but also just and equitable.

Case Studies in Bias and Fairness

Healthcare Diagnostics

A diagnostic AI tool trained on data predominantly from one demographic might underperform when applied to a more diverse population. By incorporating data from multiple sources and applying fairness-aware algorithms, researchers can improve the tool's accuracy across different groups, ultimately leading to better health outcomes for all patients.

Credit Scoring

In finance, biased credit scoring algorithms can limit access to loans for certain minority groups. Companies are now using fairness metrics to evaluate these models and adjusting their algorithms to ensure that credit decisions are based on relevant financial behavior rather than demographic factors.

Criminal Justice

Predictive policing systems have faced criticism for reinforcing existing biases in law enforcement. By implementing transparent data collection practices, auditing algorithms for bias, and involving community stakeholders, cities are working to create systems that are both effective in crime prevention and respectful of civil rights.

The Future of Fair AI

The journey toward fair and unbiased AI is ongoing and requires constant vigilance. As AI systems become more integrated into every aspect of our lives, ensuring fairness will remain a critical challenge and opportunity.

- **Regulatory and Policy Frameworks:**
  Governments and international organizations are increasingly recognizing the need for regulations that promote fairness and transparency in AI. Clear policies can set standards for ethical AI deployment across industries.

- **Technological Advancements:**
  Ongoing research in explainable AI and fairness-aware machine learning promises to provide new tools and techniques for mitigating bias. As these methods mature, we can expect AI systems to become more equitable and reliable.

- **Cultural and Ethical Shifts:**
  Ultimately, achieving fairness in AI will require not only technical solutions but also a cultural shift toward valuing diversity, inclusivity, and ethical responsibility in technology development.

Conclusion

Bias and fairness are not peripheral issues in AI—they are central to ensuring that technology serves all segments of society equitably. By understanding the sources of bias, defining what fairness means in context, and implementing robust strategies to mitigate inequities, developers can build AI systems that are both powerful and just.

As you continue your exploration of artificial intelligence, remember that the true measure of progress is not only in technological breakthroughs but also in the positive impact these innovations have on humanity. Ethical AI is a commitment to fairness, transparency, and accountability—a commitment that will shape the future of technology in ways that uplift and empower every individual.

Welcome to the evolving landscape of equitable AI—where every line of code is an opportunity to create a fairer, more inclusive world.

Chapter 17: AI and the Future of Work

Artificial Intelligence is reshaping the way we work, from automating routine tasks to creating entirely new industries and job roles. As AI continues to evolve, its impact on the workforce is both transformative and complex. In this chapter, we explore how AI is altering traditional work environments, the balance between job displacement and creation, the need for upskilling and reskilling, and the ethical considerations that accompany these changes. Join us as we examine the evolving landscape of work in an AI-driven world.

The Changing Nature of Work

Automation and Efficiency

One of the most visible effects of AI on work is its ability to automate routine and repetitive tasks.

- **Streamlining Processes:**
  AI-powered systems can process data, manage schedules, and even handle customer inquiries around the clock, allowing human employees to focus on higher-level decision-making and creative problem-solving.

- **Enhanced Productivity:**
  Automation reduces the likelihood of human error, speeds up task execution, and enables businesses

to operate more efficiently. For example, AI-driven chatbots can handle thousands of customer interactions simultaneously, freeing human agents to address more complex issues.

New Job Roles and Industries

While automation may eliminate some traditional roles, AI is also a powerful catalyst for job creation and innovation.

- **Emerging Fields:**
  New industries are arising around AI technology, including data science, machine learning engineering, and AI ethics consulting. These roles require specialized skills that did not exist a decade ago.

- **Hybrid Roles:**
  Many existing jobs are evolving into hybrid roles that combine domain expertise with technical skills. For instance, marketing professionals are now expected to analyze data trends and collaborate with AI tools to create targeted campaigns.

- **Creative and Strategic Opportunities:**
  As machines take over routine tasks, human workers have more time to focus on strategic planning, innovation, and creative pursuits—areas where human intuition and creativity remain unmatched.

Job Displacement vs. Job Creation

The Displacement Debate

AI's ability to automate tasks has led to concerns about widespread job displacement.

- **Routine Tasks at Risk:**
  Jobs that involve predictable and repetitive tasks are most vulnerable to automation. Manufacturing, administrative support, and even certain aspects of customer service have seen significant shifts due to AI integration.

- **Regional and Sectoral Impact:**
  The impact of AI is not uniform across all regions or industries. While some sectors may experience significant job losses, others could see rapid growth and transformation.

Opportunities for Job Creation

History shows that technological revolutions, while disruptive, often lead to the creation of new opportunities.

- **New Industries and Markets:**
  The AI revolution is spawning entirely new sectors—such as autonomous vehicles, smart robotics, and advanced healthcare diagnostics—that demand fresh talent and skills.

- **Reshaping Traditional Roles:**
  Rather than completely eliminating jobs, AI is

changing the way many professions operate. Teachers, for instance, are now using AI-powered tools to personalize learning, and doctors are leveraging AI for more accurate diagnostics.

- **Entrepreneurial Ventures:**
  AI also lowers the barrier for starting new businesses. Startups can harness AI technologies to innovate rapidly, create niche products, and compete in global markets.

Reskilling and Upskilling: Preparing for an AI-Driven Economy

The Need for Continuous Learning

As AI transforms the workplace, the need for lifelong learning and skill development becomes paramount.

- **Bridging the Skills Gap:**
  Many traditional roles require new technical skills to work effectively alongside AI. This shift calls for targeted training programs, online courses, and vocational education tailored to the demands of modern industries.

- **Government and Corporate Initiatives:**
  Governments and companies are increasingly investing in upskilling programs. Initiatives such as coding boot camps, data literacy workshops, and

partnerships with educational institutions are critical in preparing the workforce for a future where AI is omnipresent.

Embracing Interdisciplinary Expertise

Success in an AI-driven world often depends on combining domain expertise with technical proficiency.

- **Cross-Functional Teams:**
  Organizations are creating interdisciplinary teams that blend skills in engineering, design, ethics, and business strategy. This collaborative approach ensures that AI is implemented thoughtfully and effectively.

- **Soft Skills in a Digital Age:**
  While technical skills are crucial, soft skills—such as critical thinking, creativity, and emotional intelligence—remain invaluable. These skills complement AI's capabilities and enhance human decision-making in complex situations.

AI and Remote Work

The Rise of Digital Workspaces

The global shift toward remote work, accelerated by recent events, has been further empowered by AI.

- **Virtual Collaboration Tools:**
  AI-enhanced platforms facilitate communication, project management, and collaboration across distributed teams. These tools use natural language processing to transcribe meetings, summarize discussions, and manage tasks automatically.

- **Flexible Work Arrangements:**
  AI enables companies to monitor productivity and allocate resources more effectively, fostering an environment where flexible and remote work can thrive without sacrificing efficiency.

Challenges and Opportunities in Remote Work

- **Maintaining Team Cohesion:**
  While remote work offers flexibility, it also presents challenges in building and maintaining a cohesive team culture. AI can help bridge this gap by creating virtual environments that simulate in-person interactions.

- **Balancing Work and Wellbeing:**
  The integration of AI in remote work also raises questions about work-life balance and digital fatigue. Employers must use AI responsibly to support employee wellbeing and ensure that technology enhances, rather than detracts from, quality of life.

Ethical and Societal Implications

Addressing Inequality

The deployment of AI in the workplace has the potential to exacerbate economic inequalities if not managed carefully.

- **Access to Technology:**
  Workers in under-resourced regions or industries may struggle to access the training and tools needed to transition into new roles. Equitable investment in education and technology is essential to prevent widening disparities.

- **Fair Compensation:**
  As AI increases productivity, it is important to ensure that the benefits are distributed fairly among all workers. Policies that promote fair wages and social safety nets can help mitigate the risks of job displacement.

The Role of Policy and Regulation

Government policies play a crucial role in shaping the future of work in an AI-driven economy.

- **Labor Laws and Standards:**
  Updating labor laws to protect workers in a rapidly changing technological landscape is vital. This includes ensuring fair treatment, job security, and avenues for redress in cases of displacement.

- **Ethical Guidelines for AI Deployment:**
  Policymakers must work with industry leaders to establish ethical guidelines that govern the use of AI in the workplace. Transparency, accountability, and worker participation are key principles in this process.

Looking Ahead: The Future Workforce

Emerging Trends

The integration of AI in the workplace is an ongoing process, and several trends are emerging that will shape the future workforce:

- **Hybrid Work Models:**
  A blend of remote and on-site work is likely to become the norm, with AI tools facilitating seamless transitions between different work environments.

- **Gig and Freelance Economy:**
  AI platforms are enabling more flexible work arrangements, contributing to the rise of the gig economy. This trend offers both opportunities and challenges in terms of job security and benefits.

- **Human-AI Collaboration:**
  The future will see more sophisticated partnerships between humans and machines, where AI handles data-driven tasks and humans focus on creativity,

strategy, and interpersonal interactions.

Preparing for Change

Adapting to the future of work requires proactive strategies at both the individual and organizational levels.

- **Embracing Change:**
  Workers must cultivate a mindset of lifelong learning and adaptability. Embracing new technologies and continuously updating skills will be critical in staying relevant.

- **Organizational Transformation:**
  Companies need to invest in training, create a culture of innovation, and adopt flexible work policies that leverage AI for competitive advantage while supporting employee growth.

Conclusion

AI is fundamentally altering the landscape of work, offering both unprecedented opportunities and significant challenges. From automating routine tasks to creating new industries and reshaping job roles, the impact of AI on the workforce is profound and far-reaching. As we look to the future, the key to thriving in an AI-driven economy lies in adaptability, continuous learning, and a commitment to fairness and inclusivity.

By embracing the transformative power of AI, investing in

skill development, and addressing ethical concerns head-on, individuals and organizations can navigate the evolving world of work with confidence and resilience. The future of work is not a destination but a journey—one that requires collaboration between humans and machines, and a shared vision for a more productive, equitable, and innovative society.

Welcome to the future of work—a dynamic landscape where artificial intelligence is not just a tool, but a partner in shaping a more prosperous and sustainable tomorrow.

Chapter 18: AI in Industry: Transforming Healthcare, Finance, Entertainment, and More

Artificial Intelligence is no longer confined to academic research or futuristic speculation—it has become a transformative force in a wide range of industries. From revolutionizing patient care in healthcare to reshaping investment strategies in finance and redefining storytelling in entertainment, AI is driving innovation, efficiency, and new business models. In this chapter, we explore how AI is being applied across various sectors, the benefits and challenges that arise from its integration, and the future prospects of an AI-powered industrial landscape.

AI in Healthcare

Revolutionizing Patient Care

AI is transforming healthcare by improving diagnostics, treatment, and patient outcomes.

- **Diagnostics and Medical Imaging:**
  Deep learning algorithms analyze X-rays, MRIs, and CT scans to detect anomalies with remarkable accuracy. For example, AI systems can identify early signs of diseases like cancer or diabetic retinopathy, often surpassing the diagnostic accuracy of human experts.

- **Personalized Medicine:**
  By integrating data from genomics, electronic health records, and wearable devices, AI helps create personalized treatment plans. Predictive analytics enable physicians to tailor therapies based on an individual's genetic makeup and lifestyle, optimizing efficacy and reducing adverse effects.

- **Operational Efficiency:**
  AI streamlines hospital operations by optimizing patient scheduling, managing inventory for critical supplies, and predicting patient admissions. These improvements not only enhance patient care but also reduce costs and resource waste.

Enhancing Research and Drug Development

- **Accelerating Clinical Trials:**
  AI models analyze large datasets to identify suitable candidates for clinical trials and predict outcomes, significantly reducing the time and expense involved in drug development.

- **Discovering New Treatments:**
  Machine learning algorithms scan scientific literature and experimental data to propose novel drug candidates or identify repurposing opportunities for existing medications.

AI in Finance

Transforming Financial Services

AI is reshaping the finance industry by enhancing decision-making, automating routine tasks, and managing risk more effectively.

- **Algorithmic Trading:**
  High-frequency trading systems powered by AI analyze market data in real time to execute trades at speeds and accuracies far beyond human capabilities. These systems can identify trends, react to market fluctuations, and optimize investment strategies dynamically.

- **Risk Management and Fraud Detection:**
  AI algorithms monitor transaction patterns to detect fraudulent activities and assess credit risk. By analyzing historical data and real-time information, these systems provide early warnings and help financial institutions mitigate potential losses.

- **Personalized Financial Advice:**
  Robo-advisors use machine learning to offer tailored investment recommendations, balancing risk and reward based on an individual's financial profile and market conditions. This democratizes access to high-quality financial planning services, even for retail investors.

Improving Customer Experience

- **Chatbots and Virtual Assistants:**
  Financial institutions employ AI-powered chatbots
  to handle customer inquiries, process transactions,
  and provide account updates, thereby enhancing
  customer service while reducing operational costs.

- **Automated Loan Processing:**
  By automating credit scoring and loan approvals, AI
  reduces turnaround times and improves fairness in
  lending decisions, although it requires careful
  oversight to avoid unintended bias.

AI in Entertainment

Redefining Creativity and Content Creation

The entertainment industry is leveraging AI to generate,
personalize, and enhance creative content.

- **Content Recommendation Systems:**
  Streaming platforms such as Netflix and Spotify use
  sophisticated AI algorithms to analyze user
  behavior and preferences. This data-driven
  approach ensures that content recommendations
  are highly personalized, keeping audiences
  engaged and satisfied.

- **Generative Art and Storytelling:**
  AI models are now capable of creating original

music, visual art, and even narratives. These generative systems can serve as tools for artists, providing inspiration and novel ideas, or as autonomous creators that produce unique pieces of work.

- **Enhanced Visual Effects:**
  In film and television, AI is used to improve visual effects, automate editing processes, and even restore or colorize old footage. These advancements not only cut costs but also push the creative boundaries of what can be achieved on screen.

Interactive and Immersive Experiences

- **Virtual Reality (VR) and Augmented Reality (AR):**
  AI enhances VR and AR experiences by creating realistic simulations and adaptive environments. Whether it's for immersive gaming or interactive storytelling, AI contributes to more engaging and dynamic user experiences.

- **Personalized Advertising:**
  AI-driven analytics enable advertisers to deliver highly targeted ads based on user behavior, leading to more relevant and engaging marketing campaigns.

AI in Manufacturing and Supply Chain

Increasing Efficiency and Reducing Waste

In manufacturing and supply chain management, AI plays a critical role in streamlining operations and optimizing resources.

- **Predictive Maintenance:**
  Sensors and IoT devices collect data on machinery performance, which AI algorithms analyze to predict equipment failures before they occur. This proactive approach minimizes downtime and maintenance costs.

- **Process Optimization:**
  Machine learning models optimize production schedules, manage inventory levels, and forecast demand with high accuracy. By predicting market trends and supply chain disruptions, companies can make better-informed decisions that reduce waste and enhance profitability.

- **Quality Control:**
  AI systems inspect products on assembly lines in real time, identifying defects and ensuring that only high-quality products reach consumers. Automated visual inspection tools have become indispensable in industries where precision is critical.

AI in Retail and Customer Experience

Personalizing the Shopping Experience

Retailers are harnessing AI to create more personalized, efficient, and engaging shopping experiences.

- **Customer Insights and Behavior Analysis:**
  AI analyzes customer data—from purchase history to online browsing patterns—to identify trends and predict future behavior. This information drives targeted marketing campaigns and helps retailers tailor their product offerings.

- **Inventory and Supply Chain Management:**
  AI optimizes stock levels and predicts demand fluctuations, ensuring that products are available when and where they are needed. This minimizes stockouts and reduces excess inventory, contributing to a more sustainable retail operation.

- **In-Store Experiences:**
  AI-powered kiosks, virtual fitting rooms, and smart mirrors are transforming brick-and-mortar stores by offering interactive, personalized experiences that blend the convenience of online shopping with the tactile engagement of physical retail.

Challenges and Considerations

While AI brings significant benefits to industry, its integration also presents several challenges:

- **Data Privacy and Security:**
  Industries must balance the advantages of data-driven insights with the need to protect customer and employee information from breaches and misuse.

- **Ethical Concerns:**
  As with other areas of AI, ensuring fairness and transparency in automated decision-making is critical. Industries must address issues of bias, particularly in areas like finance and healthcare.

- **Workforce Transition:**
  The adoption of AI often leads to changes in job roles and skill requirements. Companies need to invest in reskilling programs to help employees adapt to the evolving technological landscape.

- **Regulatory Compliance:**
  As governments develop new regulations around AI, industries must stay abreast of legal requirements to ensure that their AI applications meet all necessary standards and ethical guidelines.

Looking Forward: The Future of AI in Industry

The transformative power of AI is only set to increase as technologies mature and new applications emerge. Key trends on the horizon include:

- **Edge AI and Real-Time Analytics:**
  Advances in edge computing will allow AI to process data locally on devices, reducing latency and enabling real-time decision-making in industries such as autonomous vehicles and smart manufacturing.

- **Integration Across Industries:**
  The convergence of AI with other emerging technologies—such as blockchain, quantum computing, and 5G connectivity—will create new opportunities for innovation across sectors.

- **Sustainable and Responsible AI:**
  As industries become more reliant on AI, there will be a growing focus on developing sustainable, ethical, and transparent AI systems that prioritize social good alongside economic efficiency.

Conclusion

AI is transforming industries in profound ways, driving innovation, efficiency, and personalized experiences across healthcare, finance, entertainment, manufacturing, and retail. By harnessing the power of advanced algorithms, vast data sets, and cutting-edge computing, organizations can solve complex problems, improve operational performance, and deliver unprecedented value to customers.

However, with these opportunities come challenges that require careful management—ensuring data privacy, mitigating ethical risks, and supporting workforce transitions are critical to realizing AI's full potential. As we look to the future, the continuous evolution of AI promises to reshape industry landscapes even further, forging a path toward more intelligent, sustainable, and inclusive practices.

Welcome to the era of industrial transformation powered by artificial intelligence—a future where innovation meets efficiency and every sector benefits from the revolutionary potential of AI.

Chapter 19: Debunking AI Myths and Misconceptions

Artificial Intelligence is a field that has captured the public imagination, fueled by media portrayals, science fiction, and a blend of hype and hope. With so many narratives surrounding AI, misconceptions abound. In this chapter, we will set the record straight by debunking some of the most common myths and misunderstandings about AI. By separating fact from fiction, we can gain a clearer, more realistic perspective on what AI can—and cannot—do.

The Origins of AI Myths

Before we dive into specific misconceptions, it's important to understand why these myths exist. Several factors contribute to the formation and perpetuation of AI myths:

- **Science Fiction and Pop Culture:**
  Movies, television shows, and novels often depict AI as either benevolent, all-powerful beings or as dangerous entities poised to overthrow humanity. These dramatized portrayals influence public perception and fuel unrealistic expectations.

- **Media Hype:**
  News stories sometimes focus on breakthrough achievements without fully explaining the limitations or context, leading to the idea that AI is a magical solution to all problems.

- **Complexity and Invisibility:**
  The underlying mechanisms of AI are often abstract and complex, which makes it easy for oversimplified narratives to take root. When people don't fully understand how AI works, myths can fill the void.

- **Fear of the Unknown:**
  As with any transformative technology, the uncertainty and rapid pace of change can lead to fear and skepticism, manifesting in exaggerated warnings about AI's potential risks.

Common Myths About AI

Myth 1: AI Is Sentient and Capable of Human-Like Thought

One of the most pervasive myths is that AI systems are conscious, self-aware, or capable of independent thought. This misconception is often fueled by the anthropomorphic language used to describe AI functions.

- **Reality:**
  AI systems are sophisticated tools that process data and execute programmed algorithms. They do not possess emotions, self-awareness, or consciousness. Even the most advanced models operate based on mathematical patterns and statistical probabilities, not intuition or

understanding.

Myth 2: AI Will Inevitably Lead to Massive Job Losses and Economic Collapse

Many fear that AI's automation capabilities will render human labor obsolete, causing widespread unemployment and societal disruption.

- **Reality:**
  While AI can automate routine tasks, it also creates new job opportunities and industries. Historical technological revolutions have shown that, although some roles become redundant, others emerge that require human ingenuity, creativity, and oversight. The challenge lies in managing the transition through education, reskilling, and thoughtful policy-making.

Myth 3: AI Can Solve Every Problem Instantly

Some proponents suggest that AI is a magic bullet that can quickly and easily solve complex issues ranging from climate change to healthcare.

- **Reality:**
  AI is a powerful tool, but it is not a panacea. It requires significant amounts of quality data, careful tuning, and domain-specific expertise to deliver meaningful results. Moreover, many real-world problems are multifaceted, involving social, ethical, and political dimensions that extend beyond the

capabilities of current AI technologies.

Myth 4: AI Is Always Objective and Unbiased

There is a common belief that machines, being non-human, are inherently objective and free from the biases that affect human decision-making.

- **Reality:**
  AI systems learn from historical data, which can contain biases and prejudices. Without careful design and continuous monitoring, AI can perpetuate or even exacerbate these biases. It is crucial to develop and deploy AI systems with fairness and transparency in mind to mitigate these issues.

Myth 5: AI Will Soon Surpass Human Intelligence and Dominate the World

Doomsday scenarios, such as the singularity or AI takeover, are frequently discussed in both popular culture and fringe academic circles.

- **Reality:**
  While AI is advancing rapidly in specialized tasks, we are still far from achieving artificial general intelligence (AGI)—a level of cognitive ability comparable to human intelligence across all domains. Most AI applications today are designed for specific functions and lack the broad understanding required to challenge human

oversight.

The Reality of AI: What It Is and What It Isn't

Understanding what AI truly entails helps demystify the technology and place it in proper context.

AI as a Tool

- **Task-Specific Intelligence:**
  Modern AI excels at specific, well-defined tasks. Whether it's image recognition, language translation, or playing chess, AI systems are designed to perform particular functions with impressive accuracy. They do not "think" about the world in the human sense but process inputs based on pre-defined algorithms and learned patterns.

- **Data-Driven Processes:**
  AI's performance is heavily dependent on the quality and quantity of the data it is trained on. Its ability to generalize is limited by the diversity and representativeness of that data.

Limitations and Challenges

- **Interpretability:**
  Many advanced AI models, especially deep neural networks, operate as "black boxes," meaning their decision-making processes are not easily understood by humans. This lack of transparency

poses challenges in critical applications where explainability is crucial.

- **Dependence on Human Oversight:**
  Despite their capabilities, AI systems require human oversight to set objectives, define ethical boundaries, and intervene when necessary. Human judgment remains an essential component of the AI ecosystem.

- **Technical and Ethical Hurdles:**
  From ensuring data privacy to mitigating bias, significant technical and ethical challenges remain in the development and deployment of AI. These hurdles necessitate continuous research, regulation, and public dialogue.

Moving Beyond the Myths

Educating the Public

A well-informed public is essential for a balanced understanding of AI. Educational initiatives, transparent communication from researchers, and responsible media reporting can help demystify AI and dispel unfounded fears.

Responsible Innovation

Developers and companies must strive to create AI systems that are robust, transparent, and ethical. This involves rigorous testing, continuous monitoring for bias, and an openness to collaboration with experts from diverse fields including ethics, sociology, and law.

Collaborative Governance

Policymakers, industry leaders, and civil society must work together to establish guidelines and regulations that ensure AI benefits all segments of society. By fostering an inclusive dialogue about AI's role, we can address both the potential and the limitations of the technology.

Conclusion

Debunking AI myths is not about diminishing the transformative potential of the technology; rather, it is about cultivating a realistic, informed perspective that recognizes both its capabilities and its limitations. AI is a powerful tool built on data and algorithms, designed to augment human efforts—not replace human judgment or creativity.

As we navigate an increasingly AI-driven world, dispelling myths allows us to focus on genuine challenges and opportunities. By fostering education, responsible development, and collaborative governance, we can harness AI's potential to drive positive change while ensuring that its deployment is fair, transparent, and aligned with societal values.

Welcome to a clearer, more balanced view of artificial intelligence—a view that embraces its promise while acknowledging its complexities. In understanding what AI truly is, we take an important step toward unlocking the intelligence of tomorrow in a way that benefits everyone.

Chapter 20: Tools of the Trade: A Beginner's Guide to AI Software and Platforms

Embarking on your journey into artificial intelligence is exciting, but it can also feel overwhelming given the vast array of tools and platforms available today. This chapter is designed to demystify the software and platforms that form the backbone of AI development. Whether you're a hobbyist, a student, or a professional seeking to upskill, understanding these tools will empower you to start experimenting, building, and innovating in the world of AI.

The AI Software Landscape

AI software spans a wide spectrum, from programming libraries that implement complex algorithms to integrated platforms that streamline the entire process of data handling, model training, and deployment. Here's an overview of the major categories:

- **Programming Languages:**
  Languages such as Python and R are widely used in AI for their readability, extensive libraries, and strong community support. Python, in particular, has become the language of choice due to its simplicity and the breadth of AI-specific packages available.

- **Frameworks and Libraries:**
  These are pre-built collections of code that simplify complex tasks like neural network construction,

data manipulation, and statistical analysis. They allow developers to focus on solving problems rather than reinventing basic algorithms.

- **Integrated Development Environments (IDEs) and Notebooks:**
  Tools like Jupyter Notebook and PyCharm provide interactive environments where you can write code, visualize data, and document your process—all essential for rapid experimentation and learning.

- **Cloud Platforms:**
  Providers such as Amazon Web Services (AWS), Google Cloud Platform (GCP), and Microsoft Azure offer robust infrastructure for training large models, managing data, and deploying AI applications at scale.

Key Programming Languages for AI

Python

- **Why Python?**
  Python's syntax is intuitive and its community is vast. With libraries like NumPy for numerical computation, Pandas for data manipulation, and Matplotlib for visualization, Python is a one-stop-shop for AI development.

- **Popular AI Libraries:**

  - **TensorFlow:** Developed by Google, this open-source framework is highly versatile and used in both research and production environments.

  - **PyTorch:** Known for its dynamic computation graphs, PyTorch has gained popularity for its ease of use in prototyping and research.

  - **Scikit-learn:** Ideal for traditional machine learning tasks, Scikit-learn provides tools for data mining and data analysis with a focus on simplicity and efficiency.

R

- **Why R?**
  While traditionally used for statistics and data analysis, R is also making inroads into machine learning and AI, particularly in academic and research settings.

- **Key Features:**
  R offers excellent data visualization capabilities and a rich ecosystem of packages for statistical modeling, which are valuable when exploring datasets before applying more complex AI models.

AI Frameworks and Libraries

Deep Learning Frameworks

- **TensorFlow:**
  TensorFlow is an end-to-end platform that supports everything from model building and training to deployment. Its ecosystem includes TensorBoard for visualization and TensorFlow Lite for mobile and embedded systems.

- **PyTorch:**
  PyTorch is favored for its dynamic computational graph, which allows developers to change network behavior on the fly. This makes it particularly well-suited for research and rapid prototyping. Its integration with libraries like TorchVision and fastai further simplifies common tasks.

Machine Learning Libraries

- **Scikit-learn:**
  This library provides simple and efficient tools for data mining and data analysis. It covers a wide range of machine learning algorithms including classification, regression, clustering, and dimensionality reduction.

- **XGBoost and LightGBM:**
  These libraries specialize in gradient boosting—a powerful technique for building predictive models. They are known for their performance and

efficiency in handling large datasets.

Natural Language Processing (NLP) Libraries

- **NLTK (Natural Language Toolkit):**
  NLTK is one of the oldest libraries for working with human language data in Python, offering tools for text processing, classification, tokenization, stemming, tagging, parsing, and semantic reasoning.

- **spaCy:**
  Designed for production use, spaCy is known for its speed and efficiency in processing large volumes of text. It supports advanced NLP tasks like named entity recognition and dependency parsing.

- **Transformers by Hugging Face:**
  This library provides state-of-the-art pre-trained models for tasks such as translation, summarization, and text generation. Its easy-to-use interface has made it a go-to tool for developers working on language models.

Integrated Development Environments and Notebooks

Jupyter Notebook

- **Interactive Environment:**
  Jupyter Notebook is an open-source web application that allows you to create and share

documents containing live code, equations, visualizations, and narrative text. It's ideal for exploratory data analysis and machine learning experimentation.

- **Benefits:**
  With its cell-based structure, you can write, run, and test code in small increments, making it easier to debug and understand complex AI workflows.

PyCharm

- **Full-Featured IDE:**
  PyCharm is a powerful IDE specifically for Python development. It offers robust debugging tools, code analysis, and integrations with version control systems.

- **Why Choose PyCharm:**
  For larger projects or production-level code, PyCharm provides a more structured environment than Jupyter, helping maintain code quality and manage dependencies effectively.

Cloud Platforms for AI

Amazon Web Services (AWS)

- **Services Offered:**
  AWS offers a suite of AI and machine learning services, including SageMaker for building,

training, and deploying machine learning models, and DeepLens for deep learning-enabled video analytics.

- **Scalability:**
  With AWS, you can leverage scalable cloud computing resources, making it easier to train models on large datasets without investing in expensive hardware.

Google Cloud Platform (GCP)

- **AI Tools and Services:**
  GCP provides tools like AI Platform for end-to-end machine learning workflows, AutoML for building high-quality models with minimal expertise, and BigQuery for handling large-scale data analytics.

- **Integration:**
  Google's expertise in AI research is reflected in GCP's offerings, making it a popular choice for those who want to work with cutting-edge AI models and techniques.

Microsoft Azure

- **Comprehensive AI Offerings:**
  Azure offers Cognitive Services for pre-built APIs in vision, speech, language, and decision-making, as well as Azure Machine Learning for custom model development.

- **Enterprise-Ready:**
  With robust security, compliance, and integration with other Microsoft tools, Azure is well-suited for enterprise-level AI applications.

Getting Started with AI Projects

Choosing Your Tools

When beginning an AI project, consider the following:

- **Project Scope:**
  For smaller, experimental projects, tools like Jupyter Notebook with Scikit-learn or PyTorch might be sufficient. For enterprise projects, cloud platforms like AWS or Azure provide the necessary scalability.

- **Learning Curve:**
  Beginners might find Python and its associated libraries more accessible due to extensive community support and learning resources.

Building a Simple AI Model

1. **Define the Problem:**
   Start with a well-defined problem that you want to solve, whether it's predicting housing prices, classifying images, or generating text.

2. **Gather and Preprocess Data:**
   Use Pandas and NumPy to load and clean your data. Visualize it with libraries like Matplotlib or Seaborn to gain insights.

3. **Select a Model:**
   For beginners, a simple linear regression or classification model from Scikit-learn is a good start. As you gain confidence, explore more complex models like neural networks using TensorFlow or PyTorch.

4. **Train and Evaluate:**
   Split your data into training and testing sets. Train your model, evaluate its performance using appropriate metrics, and iterate on your design as needed.

5. **Deploy:**
   Once satisfied with your model, consider deploying it using cloud services or containerization tools like Docker to make it accessible to end users.

Resources for Learning and Experimentation

- **Online Courses:**
  Platforms such as Coursera, edX, and Udacity offer courses on AI and machine learning that cover both theoretical concepts and practical applications using these tools.

- **Tutorials and Documentation:**
  The official documentation for TensorFlow, PyTorch, and other libraries is an invaluable resource. Websites like Kaggle also offer hands-on projects and competitions that can help you practice and refine your skills.

- **Community Forums:**
  Engage with communities on GitHub, Stack Overflow, and AI-specific forums to seek advice, share projects, and collaborate with others who are on the same journey.

Conclusion

The tools and platforms covered in this chapter are the building blocks of your AI journey. They empower you to move from theoretical understanding to practical implementation, enabling you to experiment, learn, and innovate. Whether you choose to work locally with Python and Jupyter Notebooks or leverage the scalable power of cloud platforms, the key is to start small, build incrementally, and continuously explore new possibilities.

By familiarizing yourself with these tools of the trade, you're taking the first concrete steps toward unlocking the intelligence of tomorrow. Embrace the learning process, experiment boldly, and remember that every expert was once a beginner.

Welcome to the world of AI development—a dynamic landscape where the right tools not only make complex problems manageable but also open up endless opportunities for creativity, innovation, and transformation.

Chapter 21: Building Your Own AI Project

One of the most exciting aspects of artificial intelligence is that you don't have to be a professional researcher or data scientist to begin experimenting with it. In this chapter, we'll guide you step-by-step through the process of building your very own AI project. Whether your goal is to solve a practical problem, explore a new hobby, or simply learn by doing, this chapter will provide you with a roadmap—from defining your project and gathering data to choosing the right tools, building a model, and deploying your solution.

---

1. Defining Your Problem and Setting Goals

Every successful AI project starts with a clear understanding of what you want to achieve. Consider these questions to help define your project:

- **What Problem Are You Trying to Solve?**
  Identify a specific, well-defined problem. It could be as straightforward as classifying images of handwritten digits or as ambitious as predicting trends in stock prices.

- **What Is the Desired Outcome?**
  Determine what success looks like. Do you want a model that can accurately classify data, generate text, or perhaps recommend products? Set measurable goals (e.g., target accuracy, response

time) to help track your progress.

- **Who Is the Audience?**
  Consider who will benefit from your project. Is it for your personal learning, a community of enthusiasts, or a potential business application? Understanding your audience can guide the complexity and features of your solution.

---

2. Gathering and Preparing Data

Data is the lifeblood of any AI project. Depending on your problem, you might need to collect, clean, and label a dataset.

Finding or Creating a Dataset

- **Public Datasets:**
  Look for datasets available online on platforms like Kaggle, UCI Machine Learning Repository, or government open data portals. For example, the MNIST dataset for handwritten digits or the Iris dataset for classification tasks are great starting points.

- **Custom Data Collection:**
  If public datasets don't meet your needs, consider collecting your own data. This might involve web scraping, using APIs, or capturing sensor data. Ensure that you have permission to use and share

the data.

Data Cleaning and Preprocessing

- **Cleaning:**
  Remove duplicate entries, handle missing values, and correct errors to ensure your data is reliable.

- **Normalization:**
  Standardize your data (e.g., scaling numerical values) to improve model performance.

- **Feature Engineering:**
  Identify which features (or variables) are most relevant to your problem. This might involve creating new features from raw data or reducing the dimensionality with techniques like Principal Component Analysis (PCA).

---

3. Choosing the Right Algorithm and Tools

The selection of algorithms and tools depends largely on your problem type and the data you have.

Matching the Problem to a Technique

- **Classification and Regression:**
  If your task involves predicting a category (classification) or a continuous value (regression), consider starting with simpler models like logistic regression, decision trees, or even support vector

machines.

- **Deep Learning:**
  For tasks like image recognition, natural language processing, or tasks with large amounts of unstructured data, neural networks and deep learning frameworks like TensorFlow or PyTorch might be more appropriate.

- **Clustering and Unsupervised Learning:**
  For tasks where you need to discover hidden patterns or group similar items, algorithms like K-means or hierarchical clustering are useful.

Selecting the Tools

- **Programming Languages:**
  Python is the most popular language for AI due to its simplicity and the availability of robust libraries.

- **Libraries and Frameworks:**
  Use libraries such as Scikit-learn for classical machine learning models, TensorFlow or PyTorch for deep learning, and Pandas for data manipulation.

- **Development Environments:**
  Start with Jupyter Notebook for interactive experimentation or choose an IDE like PyCharm for larger projects.

4. Building and Training Your Model

Once you've set up your environment and prepared your data, it's time to build your model.

Model Building Steps

1. **Define the Model Architecture:**
   Based on your chosen algorithm, define the structure of your model. For a neural network, this means specifying the number of layers, neurons per layer, and activation functions.

2. **Split the Data:**
   Divide your dataset into training, validation, and testing subsets. This helps ensure that your model generalizes well to new, unseen data.

3. **Training:**
   Feed the training data into your model and let it learn. Use techniques like gradient descent for optimization, and monitor training progress using metrics such as loss and accuracy.

4. **Validation and Tuning:**
   Evaluate your model on the validation set and adjust hyperparameters (e.g., learning rate, number of epochs, batch size) as needed. This iterative process helps you refine your model.

Tools for Model Evaluation

- **Visualization:**
  Libraries such as Matplotlib and Seaborn can help you visualize training progress, performance metrics, and error distributions.

- **Metrics:**
  Depending on your problem, common metrics include accuracy, precision, recall, F1 score for classification, and mean squared error for regression.

---

5. Evaluating, Iterating, and Refining

After training, it's important to evaluate your model's performance thoroughly.

- **Testing on Unseen Data:**
  Use your test dataset to assess how well your model performs on new data. This step is crucial to avoid overfitting.

- **Error Analysis:**
  Examine the cases where your model fails. Understanding these errors can provide insights into potential improvements, such as gathering more data or tweaking the model architecture.

- **Iteration:**
  Building an AI project is rarely a one-shot process.

Use the insights from evaluation to iterate on your model, whether by trying a different algorithm, adjusting hyperparameters, or refining your data preprocessing steps.

6. Deploying Your AI Project

Once you are satisfied with your model, the next step is to deploy it so that it can be used in real-world applications.

Deployment Options

- **Local Deployment:**
  For small projects or prototypes, you might deploy your model locally on your computer or a dedicated server.

- **Cloud Deployment:**
  Cloud platforms like AWS, GCP, or Microsoft Azure offer services to host and scale your AI model. Tools like Flask or FastAPI can wrap your model in a web API for easy integration with other applications.

- **Mobile and Edge Deployment:**
  For applications that need to run on mobile devices or at the edge, consider using TensorFlow Lite or ONNX, which are optimized for resource-constrained environments.

Monitoring and Maintenance

- **Performance Monitoring:**
  After deployment, continuously monitor your model's performance to ensure it remains effective as new data comes in.

- **Updating the Model:**
  AI models may need retraining or fine-tuning as the underlying data distribution changes over time. Establish a maintenance plan for periodic updates.

---

7. A Real-World Example: Handwritten Digit Recognition

Let's consider a concrete example: building a model to recognize handwritten digits using the MNIST dataset.

1. **Problem Definition:**
   The goal is to classify images of handwritten digits (0-9) with high accuracy.

2. **Data Preparation:**
   Use the MNIST dataset, which contains 60,000 training images and 10,000 test images, preprocessed into a consistent format.

3. **Model Selection:**
   A simple convolutional neural network (CNN) is ideal for this image classification task.

4. **Training:**

   Train the CNN using a framework like TensorFlow or PyTorch, monitoring accuracy and loss on a validation set.

5. **Evaluation:**

   Once trained, evaluate the model on the test set to ensure it generalizes well.

6. **Deployment:**

   Deploy the model as a web service so that users can upload an image and receive a digit prediction.

This example illustrates the end-to-end process of building, evaluating, and deploying an AI project, providing a blueprint that can be adapted to other problems.

---

8. Resources for Further Learning

Building your own AI project is a learning process that benefits from community and continued education. Consider these resources:

- **Online Courses:**

  Platforms like Coursera, Udacity, and edX offer courses on machine learning and AI projects that include hands-on assignments.

- **Tutorials and Workshops:**

  Websites such as Kaggle and Medium host

numerous tutorials and case studies that guide you through specific projects.

- **Community Forums:**
  Engage with communities on GitHub, Stack Overflow, and specialized AI forums to ask questions, share progress, and collaborate with others.

- **Books:**
  Titles like *"Hands-On Machine Learning with Scikit-Learn, Keras, and TensorFlow"* offer practical, project-based approaches to learning AI.

Conclusion

Building your own AI project is an empowering way to apply theoretical knowledge in a practical context. From defining the problem and gathering data to selecting the right tools, building the model, and deploying your solution, each step is a learning opportunity that brings you closer to mastering the intelligence of tomorrow.

As you embark on your project, remember that experimentation, iteration, and community engagement are key. Every challenge you encounter is a chance to learn and improve. With persistence and curiosity, you'll not only build a successful AI project but also develop the skills and insights necessary to innovate in this rapidly evolving field.

Welcome to the journey of creating your own AI project—a hands-on adventure where ideas come to life through code, data, and creativity. Embrace the process, and let each step inspire you to push the boundaries of what's possible with artificial intelligence!

Chapter 22: AI Safety and the Road Ahead

As artificial intelligence becomes ever more integrated into critical aspects of society, ensuring that these systems operate safely and reliably is of paramount importance. AI safety is not only about preventing unintended behavior or catastrophic failures—it's also about ensuring that AI remains aligned with human values, operates transparently, and adapts responsibly to a changing world. In this chapter, we will explore the core concepts of AI safety, examine the challenges and current research efforts, and look ahead to the evolving strategies that promise to safeguard the future of AI.

Understanding AI Safety

Defining AI Safety

At its essence, AI safety encompasses all measures, techniques, and policies designed to prevent harm from AI systems. This involves ensuring that:

- **AI Systems Behave as Intended:**
  Whether it's a recommendation engine, an autonomous vehicle, or a diagnostic tool, the system must reliably perform its designated task without causing unforeseen harm.

- **Alignment with Human Values:**
  AI must act in ways that reflect our ethical principles

and societal norms, even when operating in complex or ambiguous situations.

- **Robustness and Resilience:**
  Systems should continue to operate safely under unexpected conditions, adversarial attacks, or when confronted with data outside their training distribution.

Why AI Safety Matters

The potential impact of AI spans every sector—from healthcare and finance to national security and personal privacy. As these systems take on more autonomous roles, the consequences of failure can be significant. For example:

- In healthcare, an erroneous diagnostic system could lead to misdiagnosis and improper treatment.

- In autonomous driving, a malfunctioning system could result in accidents, endangering lives.

- In financial markets, rogue algorithms could trigger systemic risks and economic instability.

Recognizing these stakes, researchers and policymakers emphasize the need for rigorous safety protocols and continual oversight to ensure that AI technologies are deployed responsibly.

Key Challenges in AI Safety

The Black Box Problem and Interpretability

Many modern AI systems, particularly those based on deep learning, are often described as "black boxes" because their decision-making processes are difficult to interpret. This opacity raises several safety concerns:

- **Lack of Transparency:**
  When it's unclear how an AI arrives at a decision, it becomes challenging to predict and prevent errors.

- **Difficulty in Debugging:**
  Without insight into internal workings, identifying the source of a malfunction can be a complex and time-consuming process.

- **Trust and Accountability:**
  Stakeholders, including end-users and regulators, need assurance that the system's behavior can be audited and explained.

Robustness Against Adversarial Attacks

Adversarial attacks involve intentionally manipulating inputs to an AI system to produce incorrect outputs. For instance:

- **Image Recognition:**
  Subtle alterations to an image—imperceptible to humans—can cause an AI system to misclassify the image entirely.

- **Autonomous Systems:**
  Malicious interference with sensor data could lead to incorrect decisions in real time, potentially resulting in dangerous situations.

Developing AI systems that can resist such attacks is a critical research area, requiring methods for detecting, mitigating, and recovering from adversarial inputs.

Alignment with Human Values

A fundamental challenge in AI safety is ensuring that AI systems act in accordance with human values and ethical principles. This challenge, often referred to as the alignment problem, involves:

- **Value Specification:**
  Clearly defining the objectives and constraints that an AI system must respect.

- **Complexity of Human Values:**
  Human values are diverse, context-dependent, and sometimes conflicting, making it difficult to encode them in a machine-understandable format.

- **Dynamic Environments:**
  As societal norms and values evolve over time, AI systems must adapt without compromising safety or fairness.

Unintended Consequences and Emergent Behavior

AI systems are typically designed with a specific goal in mind, but when deployed in real-world environments, they may exhibit unintended behaviors:

- **Optimization Pitfalls:**
  An AI system might find an unanticipated loophole in its objective function that maximizes a reward in ways that are harmful or counterproductive.

- **Emergent Complexity:**
  In multi-agent systems or large-scale networks, interactions between AI components can lead to behaviors that were not foreseen during the design phase.

Anticipating and mitigating these unintended consequences requires comprehensive testing, simulation, and the development of robust safety frameworks.

Strategies and Approaches to Enhance AI Safety

Formal Verification and Testing

One promising approach to AI safety is formal verification, which involves mathematically proving that a system meets specific safety criteria. This method is especially valuable in:

- **Critical Systems:**

  Applications in healthcare, aviation, and nuclear energy, where failure is not an option, can benefit from rigorous formal methods.

- **Simulation Environments:**

  Testing AI systems in simulated settings helps researchers identify potential failure modes and refine algorithms before real-world deployment.

Explainable AI (XAI)

Improving the interpretability of AI systems is essential for building trust and ensuring safe operation. Techniques in explainable AI include:

- **Feature Attribution:**

  Methods that identify which features most influenced a decision, providing insights into the reasoning behind an output.

- **Simplified Models:**

  Creating simpler surrogate models that approximate the behavior of more complex systems can help in understanding and auditing decisions.

- **Visualization Tools:**

  Tools that graphically represent the internal workings of neural networks can make it easier to spot anomalies and potential risks.

Robustness and Adversarial Training

Enhancing the robustness of AI systems involves designing algorithms that can withstand adversarial perturbations and unexpected inputs:

- **Adversarial Training:**
  Exposing models to adversarial examples during the training phase can improve their resilience against such attacks.

- **Redundancy and Fail-Safes:**
  Incorporating redundant systems and backup protocols ensures that if one component fails, others can take over to maintain safe operation.

- **Continuous Monitoring:**
  Implementing real-time monitoring and anomaly detection helps in quickly identifying and responding to unexpected behavior.

Ethical Frameworks and Policy Measures

Beyond technical solutions, a holistic approach to AI safety includes ethical guidelines and regulatory oversight:

- **Interdisciplinary Collaboration:**
  Combining insights from computer science, ethics, law, and social sciences can lead to more comprehensive safety standards.

- **Regulatory Policies:**
  Governments and international bodies are

increasingly focusing on creating frameworks that mandate transparency, accountability, and rigorous safety testing for AI systems.

- **Public Engagement:**
  Involving diverse stakeholders in the discussion about AI safety ensures that the technology reflects broad societal values and addresses public concerns.

The Road Ahead: Future Directions in AI Safety

As AI technologies evolve, so too must the strategies for ensuring their safe deployment. Key areas for future research and development include:

- **Scalable Safety Solutions:**
  As AI systems grow more complex and are deployed at scale, developing safety protocols that can be applied broadly and efficiently will be critical.

- **Real-Time Adaptive Safety Measures:**
  Future systems may incorporate dynamic safety measures that adjust in real time to changing conditions and new data, enhancing resilience and responsiveness.

- **Integration with Emerging Technologies:**
  The convergence of AI with technologies like

quantum computing and blockchain presents new challenges—and opportunities—for safety. Research in these areas will be essential to ensure that integrated systems are secure and reliable.

- **Global Standards and Cooperation:** Establishing internationally recognized safety standards and fostering collaboration across borders will help ensure that AI technologies are developed and deployed responsibly worldwide.

Conclusion

AI safety is a multifaceted challenge that lies at the heart of responsible AI development. As our reliance on AI grows, ensuring that these systems are robust, transparent, and aligned with human values becomes ever more critical. By addressing issues of interpretability, adversarial robustness, alignment, and unintended consequences through both technical innovation and thoughtful policy, we can pave the way for a future where AI serves as a safe and beneficial partner to humanity.

The road ahead is both challenging and promising. Through rigorous research, interdisciplinary collaboration, and proactive governance, we can build AI systems that not only perform powerful functions but do so in a way that safeguards human welfare and upholds ethical standards.

Welcome to the frontier of AI safety—a vital, evolving field that will shape the trajectory of technological progress and ensure that the intelligence of tomorrow is built on a foundation of trust, resilience, and shared human values.

Chapter 23: Emerging Trends and the Future of AI

As artificial intelligence continues to advance at a breakneck pace, new trends are emerging that promise to redefine the boundaries of technology and transform industries in unprecedented ways. In this chapter, we explore the latest trends shaping AI research, development, and application. We'll examine cutting-edge innovations—from quantum computing to edge AI—and discuss how these developments will influence our technological landscape, ethical frameworks, and everyday lives in the years to come.

The Evolution of AI Research

1. Self-Supervised and Unsupervised Learning

While traditional machine learning has largely relied on large amounts of labeled data, recent breakthroughs in self-supervised and unsupervised learning are changing the game.

- **Self-Supervised Learning:**
  This approach enables AI systems to learn useful representations of data without extensive human labeling. By leveraging inherent patterns in the data, models can pre-train on vast amounts of unlabeled information and then be fine-tuned for specific tasks.

- **Unsupervised Learning Advances:**
  New algorithms are emerging that can discover complex structures and relationships in data autonomously. These methods promise to reduce dependency on labeled datasets and open up AI to domains where annotated data is scarce.

2. Reinforcement Learning and Autonomous Agents

Reinforcement learning (RL) continues to evolve, with research pushing its boundaries to handle more complex, dynamic environments.

- **Hierarchical Reinforcement Learning:**
  By decomposing complex tasks into simpler subtasks, hierarchical RL allows agents to learn more effectively and make decisions at multiple levels of abstraction.

- **Multi-Agent Systems:**
  The study of systems in which multiple AI agents interact is gaining traction, particularly in simulations of economic models, robotics, and even collaborative problem-solving.

- **Real-World Deployment:**
  As RL methods mature, we're witnessing their application in increasingly critical areas—ranging from autonomous vehicles navigating unpredictable urban landscapes to robotic systems that learn to collaborate safely with humans.

3. Quantum Computing and AI

Quantum computing represents a frontier where physics meets computer science, promising to exponentially speed up certain computations.

- **Quantum Machine Learning:**
  Researchers are investigating how quantum algorithms can accelerate machine learning tasks such as optimization and pattern recognition, potentially solving problems that are intractable for classical computers.

- **Hybrid Classical-Quantum Systems:**
  In the near term, a hybrid approach that leverages quantum processors for specific tasks while relying on classical systems for others may offer the most practical benefits.

4. Neuromorphic Computing and Brain-Inspired Models

Inspired by the human brain, neuromorphic computing aims to mimic neural architectures and energy-efficient processing.

- **Energy Efficiency:**
  Neuromorphic chips are designed to perform complex computations with significantly lower energy consumption than traditional hardware—a crucial advantage for mobile and edge applications.

- **Real-Time Learning:**
  These systems hold the potential for real-time adaptive learning, making them ideal for applications in robotics, sensory processing, and interactive devices.

Emerging Applications and Industry Trends

1. Edge AI and the Internet of Things (IoT)

As AI moves from centralized data centers to edge devices, new possibilities for real-time, on-device intelligence are emerging.

- **Low-Latency Decision-Making:**
  Edge AI enables devices such as smartphones, smart cameras, and industrial sensors to process data locally, reducing latency and improving responsiveness in critical applications like autonomous driving and real-time health monitoring.

- **Scalability and Privacy:**
  By processing data on the device rather than sending it to the cloud, edge AI enhances user privacy and reduces the burden on network infrastructure.

2. Personalized and Predictive Medicine

In healthcare, AI is increasingly driving personalized treatment plans and predictive diagnostics.

- **Genomics and Precision Medicine:**
  AI algorithms are being used to analyze genetic information and tailor treatments to an individual's unique genetic profile, improving outcomes and reducing side effects.

- **Early Disease Detection:**
  Advanced imaging techniques, coupled with AI, are enabling the early detection of diseases such as cancer, often before symptoms manifest, which is crucial for effective intervention.

3. AI for Climate Change and Environmental Sustainability

The urgent need to address climate change has spurred innovative applications of AI in environmental monitoring and sustainability.

- **Predictive Analytics for Weather and Climate:**
  AI models help predict extreme weather events, monitor environmental changes, and optimize resource management, from energy grids to water supplies.

- **Optimizing Agriculture:**
  AI-driven precision agriculture uses data from

drones, satellites, and sensors to optimize irrigation, fertilization, and pest control, leading to more sustainable farming practices.

4. Creative and Interactive Media

AI's creative capabilities are expanding the horizons of art, music, and entertainment.

- **Generative Adversarial Networks (GANs) and Beyond:**
  New models are not only producing realistic images and videos but are also enabling novel forms of interactive storytelling, where narratives evolve based on user interaction.

- **Virtual Reality (VR) and Augmented Reality (AR):**
  AI enhances immersive experiences by creating adaptive environments in real time, blending digital and physical worlds in ways that were previously unimaginable.

Ethical, Societal, and Regulatory Considerations

1. Evolving Ethical Frameworks

As AI becomes more integrated into society, ethical considerations must evolve alongside technological advancements.

- **Transparency and Explainability:**
  Future AI systems must prioritize transparency to build trust among users and ensure accountability. Researchers are working on models that not only perform well but also explain their decision-making processes in human-understandable terms.

- **Global Collaboration on AI Ethics:**
  International bodies and governments are beginning to collaborate on ethical standards and regulatory frameworks to ensure that AI development is aligned with global values and human rights.

2. Addressing the Digital Divide

The benefits of AI should be accessible to all, not just those in technologically advanced regions.

- **Inclusive AI Development:**
  Efforts are underway to democratize AI through open-source platforms, affordable educational resources, and initiatives that bridge the digital divide between developed and developing regions.

- **Equitable Policy-Making:**
  Policymakers are tasked with ensuring that the deployment of AI does not exacerbate existing social and economic inequalities but instead contributes to a more equitable distribution of opportunities.

3. Regulatory and Legal Landscapes

As AI becomes more pervasive, regulatory measures must keep pace with technological innovation.

- **Adaptive Regulations:**
  Laws and guidelines need to be flexible enough to adapt to rapid changes in AI technology while providing clear boundaries to protect consumers and society at large.

- **International Standards:**
  The development of global standards for AI safety, ethics, and data privacy is crucial in creating a cohesive framework that facilitates innovation while safeguarding fundamental rights.

The Road Ahead: Future Directions and Possibilities

The future of AI is both exciting and unpredictable, offering vast potential while posing significant challenges. As we look to the next decade, several key trends are likely to shape the landscape:

- **Convergence of Technologies:**
  The integration of AI with other emerging technologies—such as blockchain, the Internet of Things, and quantum computing—will lead to new paradigms in security, data management, and computational efficiency.

- **From Narrow to General Intelligence:**
  Although true artificial general intelligence (AGI) remains a distant goal, incremental advances in broadening the capabilities of AI systems will continue to push the boundaries of what machines can do.

- **Sustainable AI Development:**
  As environmental concerns mount, the focus on developing energy-efficient, sustainable AI systems will intensify, driving innovations in hardware, algorithms, and operational practices.

- **Human-AI Collaboration:**
  The future of work and creativity will be defined by a seamless collaboration between humans and AI, where machines augment human capabilities rather than replace them.

Conclusion

Emerging trends in AI research and applications are setting the stage for a future that is both technologically advanced and deeply transformative. From breakthroughs in self-supervised learning and quantum computing to the integration of AI at the edge and in sustainable practices, the next phase of AI promises to reshape industries, enhance human capabilities, and address some of the most pressing challenges of our time.

At the same time, these advances bring with them complex ethical, societal, and regulatory challenges that must be met with thoughtful, collaborative approaches. By fostering innovation that is both responsible and inclusive, we can ensure that the evolution of AI benefits all of humanity.

Welcome to the future of artificial intelligence—a dynamic, interconnected landscape where emerging trends and cutting-edge research converge to unlock the intelligence of tomorrow. Embrace the journey ahead, and prepare to be part of a technological revolution that will redefine what is possible in every facet of life.

Chapter 24: AI in Popular Culture: Movies, Books, and Media

Popular culture has long been fascinated with the concept of artificial intelligence, weaving it into narratives that range from awe-inspiring to cautionary. In this chapter, we explore how AI is portrayed in movies, books, television, and other media, and how these depictions shape public perception and even influence the direction of AI research. We'll examine iconic portrayals, discuss their impact on society, and consider how the gap between fiction and reality is both narrowed and widened by the stories we tell.

The Allure of AI in Storytelling

Fiction as a Mirror of Society

From the earliest days of science fiction to today's blockbuster films and streaming series, AI has served as a powerful metaphor for human hopes, fears, and ethical dilemmas. Fiction allows us to explore the consequences of technological advancements in a narrative form that is accessible and engaging. Whether it's a tale of utopia, where machines enhance human life, or a dystopia where AI threatens our existence, these stories compel us to consider the implications of creating intelligence in our own image.

- **Reflecting Human Aspirations:**
  AI in fiction often embodies our dreams of overcoming limitations—extending our reach, enhancing our capabilities, and solving problems that have long plagued humanity.

- **Highlighting Ethical Dilemmas:**
  At the same time, narratives featuring rogue or sentient machines prompt discussions about autonomy, control, and the nature of consciousness, challenging us to think about what it means to be human.

Cinematic Visions of AI

Blockbuster Films and Iconic Characters

Movies have a unique power to shape public imagination, and AI has been a central theme in many blockbuster films. Some key examples include:

- **The Terminator Series:**
  In this franchise, AI takes on a menacing form as Skynet, a self-aware defense system that deems humanity a threat and wages war against it. The portrayal raises questions about control, autonomy, and the potential dangers of unchecked technological advancement.

- **The Matrix:**

  This seminal film depicts a dystopian future where intelligent machines have enslaved humanity within a simulated reality. The Matrix challenges viewers to question the nature of reality and the relationship between human consciousness and technology.

- **Ex Machina:**

  Offering a more intimate look at AI, this film explores the relationship between a brilliant inventor, his advanced humanoid robot, and the ethical boundaries of artificial consciousness. It provokes thought on the limits of machine intelligence and the moral responsibilities of their creators.

- **Her:**

  In contrast to darker portrayals, "Her" presents a future where an AI operating system develops a deep, emotional connection with its human user. This film underscores the potential for AI to enrich our personal lives, while also highlighting the complexities of human-machine relationships.

Visual and Narrative Techniques

Filmmakers often use cutting-edge special effects, immersive sound design, and compelling narratives to bring AI to life on the big screen. These techniques not only entertain but also serve to reinforce ideas about AI's capabilities and potential risks. By visualizing complex concepts—such as self-awareness or the merging of human and machine intelligence—cinema makes abstract ideas tangible, influencing how audiences perceive the technology.

AI in Literature: From Classic Sci-Fi to Modern Narratives

Pioneering Works and Timeless Questions

Literature has long been a fertile ground for exploring AI. Classic works have set the stage for contemporary debates about technology and humanity:

- **"I, Robot" by Isaac Asimov:**
  Asimov's collection of short stories introduced the famous Three Laws of Robotics, establishing ethical guidelines for intelligent machines. His work has influenced both scientific thought and popular culture, posing enduring questions about the relationship between humans and robots.

- **"Do Androids Dream of Electric Sheep?" by Philip K. Dick:**
  The basis for the film *Blade Runner*, this novel examines the nature of consciousness and what it means to be human in a world where artificial beings are nearly indistinguishable from their creators.

- **Modern Narratives:**
  Contemporary authors continue to explore AI from various angles—ranging from optimistic visions of symbiotic relationships between humans and machines to cautionary tales about the loss of human agency in the face of overwhelming technological power.

The Role of Speculative Fiction

Speculative fiction not only entertains but also serves as a thought experiment. It challenges readers to consider scenarios that stretch the boundaries of current technology and societal norms. These narratives have a profound influence on how emerging technologies are perceived and adopted, often inspiring real-world innovations while also serving as cautionary tales.

Television, Video Games, and Digital Media

Serialized Storytelling and Episodic Exploration

Television series offer the opportunity to delve deeper into the themes of AI over multiple episodes or seasons. Series like *Westworld* and *Black Mirror* explore the multifaceted nature of AI—from the ethics of artificial consciousness to the societal impact of pervasive surveillance technologies. These shows engage audiences in long-form storytelling that allows for nuanced explorations of complex issues.

Interactive Narratives in Video Games

Video games represent another dynamic medium where AI plays a dual role:

- **Non-Player Characters (NPCs):**
  AI is used to create lifelike NPCs that adapt to player behavior, enhancing the immersion and realism of gaming worlds.

- **Procedural Storytelling:**
  Some games use AI to generate content dynamically, offering unique narratives that change with each playthrough. This interactivity blurs the line between creator and consumer, making the gaming experience deeply personal.

Social Media and AI-Driven Content

In the age of digital media, AI algorithms power content curation on platforms like YouTube, Instagram, and TikTok. These algorithms determine what content is shown to users, shaping public opinion and cultural trends. While they enhance personalization, they also raise concerns about echo chambers and the spread of misinformation.

The Impact of Popular Culture on Real-World AI

Shaping Public Perception

Popular culture plays a significant role in shaping how the public understands and reacts to AI. Overly dramatic or dystopian portrayals can lead to unrealistic fears, while utopian visions might create overly optimistic expectations about the technology's capabilities. Both extremes can influence policy decisions, funding priorities, and the direction of research.

- **Influence on Innovation:**
  Creative portrayals of AI often inspire researchers and entrepreneurs, prompting new lines of inquiry and technological development. Visionary films and novels have, in many cases, seeded ideas that later emerge as groundbreaking innovations.

- **Informing Policy and Ethics:**
  The narratives found in popular culture also inform public debates about AI ethics and regulation. They help frame discussions around accountability, privacy, and the societal implications of AI, providing a cultural context for policymaking.

Bridging Fiction and Reality

While popular culture often exaggerates or simplifies the reality of AI, it also provides a valuable platform for public engagement. Educators, scientists, and policymakers can use these cultural artifacts as starting points to explain the real workings, potential, and limitations of AI. By demystifying the technology behind the fiction, we can foster a more informed and balanced dialogue about the role of AI in our society.

Conclusion

AI in popular culture is a double-edged sword—it both reflects and shapes our collective understanding of this transformative technology. Through movies, books, television, video games, and digital media, we encounter a rich tapestry of narratives that explore the promise, peril, and profound ethical questions posed by AI. These portrayals inspire innovation, fuel debates, and sometimes even create misconceptions that must be addressed through education and thoughtful discussion.

As you continue your journey into the intelligence of tomorrow, remember that popular culture offers both cautionary tales and aspirational visions. Embracing the insights from these narratives can help guide the responsible development and deployment of AI, ensuring that it enriches our lives while remaining aligned with our values.

Welcome to the world of AI in popular culture—a realm where fiction meets reality, sparking the imagination and shaping the future of technology in profound and unexpected ways.

Chapter 25: Continuing Your AI Journey: Resources, Communities, and Lifelong Learning

Your journey into the world of artificial intelligence does not end with this book—it's only the beginning. As you move forward, the key to staying at the forefront of this rapidly evolving field is continuous learning, active community engagement, and an open mind toward new ideas and technologies. In this chapter, we provide a comprehensive guide to the resources, communities, and strategies that will support your lifelong pursuit of AI knowledge and innovation.

Embracing Lifelong Learning

The Dynamic Nature of AI

AI is an ever-changing field, with new breakthroughs, research papers, and applications emerging at a breathtaking pace. To remain effective and relevant:

- **Stay Curious:**
  Cultivate a mindset of curiosity and openness to new ideas. Be prepared to learn continuously—whether through formal education, online courses, or hands-on experimentation.

- **Adaptability:**
  As technologies evolve, the tools and techniques you learn today may be supplemented or even replaced by tomorrow's innovations. Embrace

change and view every new development as an opportunity to expand your skill set.

Creating a Personal Learning Plan

Establish a routine for learning that fits your schedule and goals:

- **Set Goals:**
  Define short-term and long-term objectives. Whether you want to master deep learning, contribute to open-source projects, or transition your career into AI, having clear goals will help guide your efforts.

- **Schedule Time:**
  Dedicate regular time for study, practice, and exploration. Consistent engagement—even if just a few hours a week—can yield significant progress over time.

- **Reflect and Adjust:**
  Periodically assess your progress and be willing to adjust your learning plan based on your interests, challenges, and the evolving AI landscape.

Online Learning Platforms and Courses

Massive Open Online Courses (MOOCs)

MOOCs have democratized access to high-quality education. Some of the most popular platforms include:

- **Coursera:**
  Offers courses from top universities and companies. Look for courses like *Machine Learning by Andrew Ng*, *Deep Learning Specialization*, or more niche topics that pique your interest.

- **edX:**
  Provides access to courses from institutions like MIT and Harvard. Courses on data science, AI ethics, and robotics can help broaden your perspective.

- **Udacity:**
  Known for its "Nanodegree" programs, Udacity offers project-based courses that focus on practical applications in AI and machine learning.

- **Khan Academy and YouTube:**
  While not exclusively for AI, these platforms offer excellent foundational content in mathematics, programming, and statistics—skills essential for advanced AI studies.

Specialized AI Learning Portals

- **fast.ai:**
  Offers a practical, hands-on approach to deep

learning that emphasizes coding and experimentation.

- **DataCamp:**
  Focused on data science and analytics, DataCamp provides interactive Python and R courses that can help you build your machine learning skills.

- **DeepLearning.AI:**
  Founded by Andrew Ng, this platform focuses on deep learning and offers a suite of courses designed to take you from beginner to expert.

Books, Journals, and Research Papers

Must-Read Books

Books are an invaluable resource for building both foundational knowledge and advanced expertise:

- *"Hands-On Machine Learning with Scikit-Learn, Keras, and TensorFlow"* by Aurélien Géron – A practical guide to implementing AI projects.

- *"Deep Learning"* by Ian Goodfellow, Yoshua Bengio, and Aaron Courville – An authoritative text on the theory and practice of deep neural networks.

- *"Artificial Intelligence: A Modern Approach"* by Stuart Russell and Peter Norvig – A comprehensive introduction to AI that covers a wide range of topics.

- *"The Hundred-Page Machine Learning Book"* by Andriy Burkov – A concise yet insightful overview of machine learning concepts.

Journals and Conferences

For those who wish to dive deeper into cutting-edge research:

- **Journals:**
  Journal of Machine Learning Research (JMLR), *IEEE Transactions on Neural Networks and Learning Systems*, and *Nature Machine Intelligence* publish high-quality research articles.

- **Conferences:**
  Attending conferences such as NeurIPS, ICML, CVPR, and ACL not only exposes you to the latest research but also provides opportunities for networking and collaboration.

Staying Current with Research

- **Preprint Servers:**
  Websites like arXiv.org host the latest research papers in AI and machine learning, often months before they appear in journals.

- **Research Blogs and Newsletters:**
  Blogs from organizations like OpenAI, DeepMind, and Google Research, as well as newsletters such as *Import AI* or *The Batch*, offer curated insights into

recent developments.

Engaging with the AI Community

Online Forums and Social Media

Active participation in online communities can accelerate your learning:

- **Stack Overflow and GitHub:**
  Engage with a vast network of developers and researchers to ask questions, share code, and collaborate on projects.

- **Reddit and LinkedIn Groups:**
  Subreddits like r/MachineLearning and various LinkedIn groups are great places to join discussions, share resources, and learn from industry experts.

- **Twitter:**
  Many AI researchers and practitioners share their insights and breakthroughs on Twitter. Following thought leaders can provide a constant stream of inspiration and knowledge.

Local Meetups and Conferences

Face-to-face interactions remain a powerful way to learn and network:

- **Meetup Groups:**
  Many cities host local AI and data science meetups where you can attend workshops, hackathons, and lectures.

- **Conferences and Workshops:**
  Even if you can't attend the major international conferences, local or regional events can offer valuable opportunities to engage with peers and professionals.

Collaborative Projects and Open-Source Contributions

Getting involved in collaborative projects can provide hands-on experience and deepen your understanding:

- **Kaggle Competitions:**
  Participate in Kaggle competitions to apply your skills in real-world scenarios and learn from the community's shared notebooks and discussions.

- **Open-Source Projects:**
  Contribute to projects on GitHub to gain practical experience, receive feedback from experienced developers, and build your professional portfolio.

Strategies for Continuous Improvement

Experimentation and Personal Projects

Nothing beats learning by doing. Build projects that interest you—even small ones can provide valuable insights:

- **Start Simple:**
  Choose a manageable project like a recommendation system, a simple chatbot, or a predictive model for a hobby-related dataset.

- **Document Your Process:**
  Maintain a blog, GitHub repository, or personal journal to document your progress. This not only reinforces your learning but also builds a portfolio that can impress future collaborators or employers.

- **Iterate and Improve:**
  Reflect on your successes and setbacks. Use each project as an opportunity to learn new techniques and refine your approach.

Seeking Mentorship and Guidance

Learning from others who have walked the path before you can accelerate your growth:

- **Find a Mentor:**
  Reach out to professionals in the field through LinkedIn, alumni networks, or local meetups. A mentor can offer advice, provide feedback, and

help you navigate career transitions.

- **Peer Learning:**
  Join study groups or collaborative projects where you can share challenges, celebrate successes, and hold each other accountable for continuous improvement.

Final Thoughts: Embracing the Journey

The field of AI is vast and ever-changing, offering endless opportunities for those willing to dive in and explore. Your journey will be marked by constant learning, experimentation, and growth. By leveraging the wealth of resources available—from online courses and books to communities and collaborative projects—you can build a robust foundation that will serve you throughout your career.

Remember, every expert was once a beginner. Stay curious, be patient, and remain open to new ideas. The landscape of AI is not static; it is a dynamic frontier that rewards those who are proactive and resilient.

Welcome to the next phase of your AI journey—a lifelong adventure filled with challenges, discoveries, and the thrill of pushing the boundaries of what is possible. Embrace the path ahead, and let the intelligence of tomorrow be shaped by your relentless pursuit of knowledge and innovation.

Appendix A: Glossary of AI Terms

Below is a comprehensive glossary of key terms and concepts that are foundational to the study of artificial intelligence. This glossary is designed to serve as a quick reference guide for readers as they navigate the world of AI. Each term is defined in clear, accessible language to help solidify your understanding of the field.

Algorithm

A step-by-step procedure or set of rules that a computer follows to perform a task or solve a problem. In AI, algorithms are used to process data and make decisions.

Artificial Intelligence (AI)

A branch of computer science focused on creating systems capable of performing tasks that normally require human intelligence, such as learning, problem-solving, and decision-making.

Big Data

Extremely large and complex datasets that traditional data processing techniques cannot handle effectively. Big Data is critical for training AI models, which require vast amounts of information to learn from.

Classification

A machine learning task where the goal is to assign data points to one or more predefined categories or classes. For example, identifying whether an email is spam or not spam.

Clustering

An unsupervised learning technique used to group similar data points together based on their features, without using labeled outcomes. Clustering helps uncover hidden patterns within data.

Computer Vision

A field of AI that focuses on enabling machines to interpret and understand visual information from the world, such as images and videos.

Data

Information, in raw or processed form, that serves as the input for AI systems. Data can be structured, semi-structured, or unstructured.

Deep Learning

A subset of machine learning that uses multi-layered neural networks to analyze various levels of data abstraction. Deep learning has been instrumental in advances in image and speech recognition.

Decision Tree

A tree-like model used for decision-making and classification that splits data into branches based on feature values, leading to a decision or classification at the end of each branch.

Ensemble Methods

Techniques that combine the predictions of multiple models to improve accuracy and robustness. Examples include Random Forests and Gradient Boosting.

Feature

An individual measurable property or characteristic of a phenomenon being observed. In AI, features are used as inputs to models.

Gradient Descent

An optimization algorithm used to minimize the loss function in machine learning models by iteratively adjusting parameters in the opposite direction of the gradient.

Hyperparameter

A configuration parameter used to structure the learning process in machine learning models. Unlike model parameters, hyperparameters are set before training begins (e.g., learning rate, number of layers).

Machine Learning (ML)

A subset of AI that focuses on developing algorithms that allow computers to learn from and make predictions or decisions based on data, without being explicitly programmed for each task.

Model

A mathematical representation of a real-world process, built using machine learning algorithms. A model learns patterns from training data and is used to make predictions on new data.

Natural Language Processing (NLP)

A field of AI that focuses on the interaction between computers and human language, enabling machines to understand, interpret, and generate text or speech.

Neural Network

A computational model inspired by the human brain's network of neurons. Neural networks consist of layers of interconnected nodes (neurons) that process data and learn patterns.

Overfitting

A modeling error that occurs when a machine learning model learns the training data too well, including its noise and outliers, resulting in poor performance on new, unseen data.

Reinforcement Learning (RL)

A type of machine learning in which an agent learns to make decisions by interacting with an environment, receiving rewards or penalties for its actions, and adjusting its behavior to maximize cumulative rewards.

Supervised Learning

A machine learning approach where the model is trained on a labeled dataset, meaning that each training example is paired with the correct output. The model learns to map inputs to outputs based on this labeled data.

Unsupervised Learning

A machine learning approach where the model is trained on unlabeled data, and the goal is to identify inherent patterns, groupings, or structures within the data.

Underfitting

A modeling error where a machine learning model is too simple to capture the underlying patterns in the data, leading to poor performance on both training and new data.

Appendix B: Further Reading and Resources

To deepen your understanding of artificial intelligence and stay current with the latest developments, here is a curated list of resources including books, online courses, websites, journals, and communities that can help you continue your AI journey.

Books

- **"Artificial Intelligence: A Modern Approach" by Stuart Russell and Peter Norvig**
  A comprehensive introduction to AI that covers both theoretical and practical aspects of the field.

- **"Hands-On Machine Learning with Scikit-Learn, Keras, and TensorFlow" by Aurélien Géron**
  A practical guide to building AI projects using popular libraries and frameworks, suitable for beginners and intermediate learners.

- **"Deep Learning" by Ian Goodfellow, Yoshua Bengio, and Aaron Courville**
  An in-depth exploration of deep learning techniques and theories, ideal for those looking to delve deeper into the subject.

- **"The Hundred-Page Machine Learning Book" by Andriy Burkov**
  A concise yet insightful overview of machine learning concepts, perfect for a quick yet comprehensive read.

Online Courses and Platforms

- **Coursera:**
  Offers courses like *Machine Learning by Andrew Ng* and deep learning specializations from top universities.

- **edX:**
  Provides courses from institutions like MIT and Harvard, covering topics in AI, data science, and robotics.

- **Udacity:**
  Known for its "Nanodegree" programs, which focus on practical, project-based learning in machine learning and AI.

- **fast.ai:**
  A platform focused on making deep learning accessible through hands-on courses that emphasize coding and experimentation.

- **DataCamp:**
  Offers interactive courses in Python and R, with a focus on data science and machine learning.

Websites and Research Platforms

- **Kaggle:**
  A community and platform for data science competitions, offering datasets, notebooks, and a vibrant community for learning and collaboration.

- **arXiv.org:**

  A preprint server where you can access the latest research papers in AI, machine learning, and related fields.

- **Towards Data Science (Medium):**

  A blog that features articles on a wide range of topics, from introductory guides to advanced AI research.

- **Official Documentation:**

  Websites like TensorFlow.org and PyTorch.org provide comprehensive documentation, tutorials, and community support for their respective frameworks.

Journals and Conferences

- **Journals:**

  Journal of Machine Learning Research (JMLR), *IEEE Transactions on Neural Networks and Learning Systems*, and *Nature Machine Intelligence* are excellent sources for cutting-edge research.

- **Conferences:**

  Events like NeurIPS, ICML, CVPR, and ACL provide opportunities to learn about the latest breakthroughs, network with experts, and gain insights into future trends in AI.

Community Engagement

- **Online Forums:**
  Platforms like Stack Overflow, Reddit (e.g., r/MachineLearning), and GitHub are great for asking questions, sharing projects, and collaborating with peers.

- **Local Meetups and Workshops:**
  Look for AI and data science meetups in your area or online webinars that offer hands-on experiences and networking opportunities.

By leveraging these resources, you can continue to expand your knowledge, stay updated with emerging trends, and actively participate in the vibrant AI community. Remember, the journey in AI is continuous—each new project, article, or discussion brings you one step closer to mastering the technology that is shaping our future.

www.ingramcontent.com/pod-product-compliance
Lightning Source LLC
LaVergne TN
LVHW021136160326
834004LV00001B/346